Pension Incentives
and
Job Mobility

Alan L. Gustman
Dartmouth College
and
National Bureau of Economic Research

Thomas L. Steinmeier
Texas Tech University

1995

W.E. Upjohn Institute for Employment Research
Kalamazoo, Michigan

Library of Congress Cataloging-in-Publication Data

Pension incentives and job mobility / Alan L. Gustman and Thomas L.
  Steinmeier.
      p. cm.
    Includes bibliographical references and index.
    ISBN 0–88099–152–6. — ISBN 0–88099–151–8 (pbk.)
    1. Pensions—Mathematical models.   2. Occupational mobility—
  Mathematical models.   I. Gustman, Alan L.   II. Steinmeier, Thomas L.
  HD7105.3.P45   1995
  331.25'2'015118—dc20   93–47534
                                                                               CIP

Copyright © 1995
W. E. Upjohn Institute for Employment Research
300 S. Westnedge Avenue
Kalamazoo, Michigan 49007–4686

Cover design by J. R. Underhill
Index prepared by Shirley Kessel.
Printed in the United States of America.

To Janice and Diane

Acknowledgments

We are grateful for support for this monograph from the W.E. Upjohn Institute for Employment Research. In addition to that support, our work on the issue of pensions and mobility has been supported by three grants from the U.S. Department of Labor and by a Martin Segal Fellowship through the Rockefeller Fund in Economics at Dartmouth College. Relevant reports submitted to the Department of Labor are entitled "Job Mobility, Older Workers and the Role of Pensions," September 1987; "Evaluating Pension Policies in a Model with Endogenous Contributions," June 1988; and "Pension Portability and Labor Mobility," October 1990. The opinions and conclusions are our own and do not represent the views of the Department of Labor, the Upjohn Institute, or any of the organizations with which we are affiliated. A technical study reporting the results of our research using data from the Survey of Income and Program Participation was published as an article entitled "Pension Portability and Labor Mobility: Evidence from the Survey of Income and Program Participation," *Journal of Public Economics*, March 1993, pp. 299-323. We thank Kevin Hollenbeck for his many helpful comments and Judith Gentry for her support in editing the manuscript.

The Authors

Alan L. Gustman is Loren M. Berry Professor of Economics at Dartmouth College and a Research Associate at the National Bureau of Economic Research. He received his Ph.D. from the University of Michigan in 1969. He currently is serving on the Steering Committee of the Health and Retirement Survey and on the Technical Advisory Panel to the National Longitudinal Survey and was Special Assistant for Economic Affairs at the U.S. Department of labor in 1976-77.

Thomas L. Steinmeier is Professor of Economics at Texas Tech University. He received his Ph.D. from Yale University in 1975 and subsequently taught at Oberlin College and Dartmouth College. He is a member of the Steering Committee of the Health and Retirement Survey, is an Adjunct Research Scientist at the University of Michigan, and is chairing the Committee on Record Linkages for the HRS, which among other things is helping in the design of pension software for evaluating employer-provided pension data.

Over the past decade and a half, Gustman and Steinmeier have written many articles together on the topics of retirement behavior, pensions, and social security. Their work has been supported by a number of federal agencies, including the National Institute on Aging, the Department of Labor through the Pension and Welfare Benefit Administration, the Office of the Assistant Secretary for Policy and the Bureau of Labor Statistics, the Social Security Administration, the Office of the Assistant Secretary for Planning and evaluation at the Department of Health and Human Services, the Department of Education, and the National Science Foundation.

Contents

List of Tables

1
Introduction and Overview

Employees whose jobs offer pensions leave their positions much less frequently than do employees whose jobs lack pensions. This observation has been confirmed by numerous researchers, working with diverse data sets covering different time periods. For instance, Allen, Clark, and McDermed (1993) found that over the seven-year period from 1975 to 1982, over 60 percent of workers not covered by pensions changed jobs. In the same time frame, less than 40 percent of workers who had pension coverage moved on to new jobs. Our own research (Gustman and Steinmeier 1993b) showed that over a one-year period between 1984 and 1985, the rate of job change among male workers without pension coverage was almost 20 percent. Meanwhile, only 6 percent of pension-covered workers switched employers.

Moreover, it does not appear that other factors, such as education or the type of job, are capable of explaining these differences in mobility rates. Even after allowing for the effects of various individual and job characteristics that might be expected to influence mobility, Mitchell (1982) found that pension-covered workers were 20 percentage points less likely to change jobs over a four-year period. This result is fairly typical. Indeed, the observation that workers with pensions move less from their jobs has come to be one of the most firmly rooted "stylized facts" in the literature dealing with pensions.

The research presented in this book challenges a widely held view as to why worker mobility is lower from jobs that offer pensions than from jobs that do not. According to that explanation, the lower mobility rate from pension-covered jobs occurs primarily because of financial disincentives created by pensions. Many pension plans use a formula to determine the amount of benefits, and the formula often increases benefits very rapidly in the final years before the specified retirement age.[1] Such plans are said to be "backloaded."[2] If workers leave the firm before qualifying for retirement, they suffer a pension "capital loss" by giving up the opportunity for substantial increases in pension benefits.[3] Thus, the prevailing view links the lower mobility of workers from pension-covered jobs and the backloading of defined benefit plans in a causal way, asserting that the capital loss from mobility discourages covered workers from leaving firms before qualifying for early retirement.

Indeed, there is a literature that takes the linkage between reduced mobility from pension-covered jobs and backloaded pensions as evidence of purposeful behavior by firms with regard to the design of pension plans. One branch of this literature argues that pensions are part of a human resource policy created to reduce the mobility of workers. Another branch argues that backloaded pensions are an integral part of compensation schemes that enhance work incentives. A further motivation attributed to the adoption of pensions is to encourage retirement at optimal ages.[4] With regard to this literature, a finding of a relationship between pensions and mobility, and especially of a negative relationship between backloaded pensions and mobility, is taken as support of a model or set of models of human resource policies in which pensions are an important tool for regulating mobility and worker productivity.

Background for Research

There are three types of evidence that have led to the belief that financial penalties from pensions reduce turnover. First, there is evidence that workers who are covered by pensions have lower rates of turnover from their jobs and longer tenure than do workers without pensions (Bartel and Borjas 1977; Mitchell 1982, 1983; and McCormick and Hughes 1984, among others). Second, as required by the theory, there are financial penalties to early mobility. Examinations of pension plans at a number of firms have revealed that the benefit formula of defined benefit plans causes the value of the pension to accrue disproportionately in the later years of employment (Bulow 1981, 1982; Kotlikoff and Wise 1985, 1987a). In addition, special benefits often accrue to those who remain with the firm until qualifying for early retirement. This research establishes the magnitude of the backloading and pension capital losses in defined benefit plans and has suggested to analysts that the resulting disincentives are sizable enough to discourage mobility. Third, there has been some recent work that has attempted to relate a measure of the disincentive to mobility in pensions directly to observed turnover behavior. That work (Allen, Clark, and McDermed 1993) has concluded that a substantial fraction of the difference in turnover associated with pension coverage is due to the loss in pension value with turnover.[5]

Our analysis confirms that turnover is lower from pension-covered jobs and that pensions are indeed structured in such a way as to result in financial penalties to early mobility. However, we do not find pension backloading to be large enough to have a strong effect on turnover, nor do we find the available evidence of the relationship between pension backloading and turnover to be persuasive as to causality. We believe that our study raises questions about the conventional view that pension backloading is responsible for the lower mobility rates of pension-covered workers.

If backloading is not the cause of lower mobility, what is? One possibility is that workers who are in pension-covered jobs are different in a way that makes them inherently more likely to remain in their jobs. These differences may or may not be observable to the investigator, but could not have been included in studies finding lower mobility from pension-covered jobs. Another possibility is that there is some aspect of pension-covered employment, other than backloading, that is responsible for reduced mobility. The explanation we favor is that workers are reluctant to leave pension-covered jobs because they receive higher compensation on those jobs than they can receive elsewhere (in the next best opportunity). This extra compensation on a pension-covered job may be called a "compensation premium."

Research Approach

Previous empirical studies have disregarded the possibility of a compensation premium, largely because the next best opportunity is not observed if the worker does not switch jobs. As a result, those studies have attributed whatever effect the compensation premium has on mobility to other variables, most notably to pensions or to pension backloading. However, we have developed a procedure that overcomes this difficulty, and we believe that the compensation premium explanation for the lower mobility rate among pension-covered workers is supported by the balance of the evidence.

The approach adopted here is more comprehensive than in the usual model, but it still does not encompass all relevant possibilities. The methodology does analyze the effects of both the degree of pension backloading and of any compensation premium on mobility. However, the model does not incorporate the possibility that backloaded pensions are used to select workers on the basis of unobservable characteristics associated with low turnover and that it is this unmeasured propensity to stay that accounts for the lower mobility of workers on pension-covered jobs. In this regard, we face the same problem as other researchers: where there are a number of potential explanations for behavior, it is often not possible to include all relevant possibilities in a single model, due to limited empirical information. The typical empirical model of mobility incorporates one or at best two of these explanations. The same is true for empirical studies explaining pension coverage, plan attributes, and pension accrual profiles and their characteristics. In all of these studies, it is hoped that the behavioral variables omitted from the analysis will be orthogonal in their impact to the included variables so that, in the absence of a relationship between included and omitted variables, coefficient estimates for included variables are unbiased. Fortunately, for the model we estimate, evidence from Allen, Clark, and McDermed (1993) suggests that selection, to the extent it exists, is based on observable, rather than unobservable, characteristics, which can be included in our analysis.

The model also does not address the source of a wage premium. In a spot labor market, where only the current period matters, and in which all agents are competitive, we can anticipate that the wage equals productivity in each period and that workers shift to jobs providing the highest benefits net of moving costs. In such a world, we would not expect to find compensation premiums. Once more realistic assumptions are adopted, however, compensation premiums may arise; these assumptions include such factors as long-term attachment of workers to firms, compensation arrangements that may span a period of time, training costs, matching workers to jobs, pockets of imperfect competition and a resulting array of rents and quasi rents, monitoring costs, imperfect and asymmetric information, and unions motivated by a variety of considerations (Krueger and Summers 1988).

The origin and even the existence of compensation premiums are intensely debated topics in the field of labor economics. Arguments abound over whether certain jobs are "good" jobs, meaning that they pay a given worker more than can be secured in other employment, or whether industry wage differentials mainly reflect compensating differentials for unmeasured factors or unmeasured ability. While there is general agreement on the existence of wage premiums on union jobs, there is, for example, disagreement on the reasons for the well-documented compensation premium that accrues to those who work at large firms (Brown and Medoff 1989). Some argue that such wage differentials are equalizing, so that those on less pleasant jobs are paid more, while others find the evidence inconsistent with an equalizing wage differentials argument. The literature also includes competing views of how wages are determined, even when there is long-term job attachment. Some argue that wage experience and wage-tenure profiles are more likely to reflect efforts by the firm to economize on the costs of specific training or on the costs of generating a good match. Others argue that the profiles reflect selection in mobility over the course of the life cycle, so that those with higher productivity are more likely to stay with the job, or even pure returns to seniority.

Research Findings

Our work does not resolve the preceding issues of wage determination or indicate a choice among the competing explanations for compensation and employment differentials. Our findings do suggest that the backloading is smaller than one would expect from a major determinant of productivity and turnover and that some aspects of the usual explanation for the effects of pensions on turnover are not consistent with observed behavior. Our results also indicate that the wage premium on pension-covered jobs has a suspiciously strong, negative relationship with the turnover observed for pension-covered workers. More specifically, the evidence that we and others have gathered suggests the following:

• The penalty to mobility from backloaded pensions is relatively small. For the average, covered male worker in his thirties or forties, the loss would be a little more than half a year's pay. If an alternative job were to pay just a few percentage points more, it would be to the worker's advantage to take the pension loss to get the higher wage. As an example, a raise of just 3 percent, multiplied by 20 years until retirement, more than offsets a pension loss of half a year's pay, especially since the increase in wages begins immediately, while the loss in pension value comes after 20 years. In general, a once-and-for-all loss of the equivalent of a few months' pay, which would be realized 20 to 30 years in the future, is not large enough to tie workers in their thirties or forties to the firm. The loss from pension backloading due to early separation is a stock rather than a flow over time, and that loss remains small relative to the wage differential from moving until the worker approaches within a decade or so of retirement age.

 • It has been suggested that firms use pensions to reduce turnover in order to lower hiring and training costs. However, the penalty to mobility from defined benefit plans is especially small for young workers. The incentives against quitting are insubstantial precisely during the time when the firm has the largest share of unrealized returns on its training investment. Until the individual reaches within about 10 years of retirement age, benefit formulas do not create a substantial penalty to leaving the firm. Thus, the evidence developed here suggests that firms would use pensions as a tool to economize on training costs only if these costs occurred throughout the period of attachment to the firm. The pension would not be helpful in economizing on the substantial fraction of training costs incurred in the initial year of hire.[6] The pension, of course, would also not be useful in economizing on hiring costs.

 • Turnover is not lower for workers who hold jobs offering backloaded pensions (mainly defined benefit pensions) than it is for workers who hold jobs offering pensions in which benefits are not backloaded (defined contribution plans). We show that, in reduced form mobility equations in which defined benefit plans are distinguished from defined contribution plans, both types of pensions are found to have an equal, negative association with the probability of turnover. Generic defined contribution plans are not backloaded, and, even with the addition of provisions that foster backloading on some defined contribution plans, such as special bonuses for those who qualify for early retirement, a nationally representative sample of defined contribution plans does not exhibit much backloading. Thus, it is a mystery as to why defined contribution plans, which are not back-loaded, should be associated with lower turnover.[7] This finding suggests that it is not the financial backloading aspect of pensions that causes lower turnover rates, but some omitted factor that is correlated both with pension coverage and with turnover.[8]

• In current empirical models relating mobility to pensions (or to pension backloading), to wages, and to other variables, the relative sizes of the pension and wage coefficients are difficult to interpret. Typically, the pension coefficient is quite large, and the wage coefficient is relatively small. Taken at face value, this would imply that the effect on mobility of having a pension is the same as that of having a very substantial wage increase. For instance, Mitchell (1982) estimates that having a pension has more effect on mobility than a tripling of the wage![9] These findings suggest to us that the current models are mis-specified if they are to be interpreted as a causal relationship. The problem is that they lack a measure of the compensation premium. If there are compensation premiums, and if those premiums are more closely correlated with pensions than with wages, then the explanatory power that should be attributed to the premiums in a mobility equation would instead be attributed to pensions. This problem would account for the pension coefficient being so large relative to the wage coefficient. In the material that follows, we develop evidence that supports this view.

• Some studies find that pensions are associated with reduced turn-over mainly because they are associated with lower layoffs, rather than lower quits (Mitchell, 1982; Allen, Clark, and McDermed 1993).[10] This finding raises questions about the motivation for adopting backloaded pensions and, in particular, about whether firms adopt backloaded pensions as a device to reduce turnover. If turnover were lower on pension-covered jobs due to a reduction in layoffs, backloaded pensions would be unnecessary as a device for lowering mobility: firms can control layoffs directly without resorting to backloaded pensions. This suggests that firms have adopted a backloaded benefit structure for other reasons, perhaps having to do with efforts to provide tax-deferred savings, to provide various types of insurance that the worker values and that are not available in the market, and/or to regulate retirement behavior (Gustman, Mitchell, and Steinmeier 1994).[11]

A finding that compensation premiums, and not pension backloading, account for reduced mobility from pension-covered jobs calls into question a number of theoretical models of the motivation for pensions. The role of backloading is central to models claiming that the defined benefit pension is a natural outgrowth of implicit contracts designed to increase worker productivity and to economize on training, supervision, and related costs. Thus, in addition to its relevance for models of worker mobility, this study is relevant to the literature on pension economics. To the degree that it uncovers additional systematic wage differentials, the study also provides evidence pertinent to models of wage determination and to the analysis of industry and compensating wage differentials.

Along with the theoretical implications, there are a number of policy implications from the finding that pension backloading *per se* is not likely to be responsible for much of the difference in mobility between workers on pension-covered and nonpension jobs. A mistaken view of causality may lead to inappropriate policies. For example, there has been some concern at the U.S. Department of Labor that pensions adversely affect productivity because they discourage mobility. This motivates a search for potential legislative cures. Some policy analysts also fear that, because of backloaded pensions, workers may stay too long with declining firms, thus worsening the positions of these firms; similarly, these analysts are concerned that workers might be reluctant to move to expanding sectors, thereby raising the labor costs of promising enterprises and inhibiting growth.[12] Legislation has required either cliff vesting—where an employee becomes fully vested after a specified number of years, with no vesting prior to that—within five years or graded vesting—where an employee is partially vested after a certain number of years and then is increasingly vested according to a schedule until attaining 100 percent vesting—within seven years (the Tax Reform Act of 1986) and has lowered the minimum age for crediting a pension to 21 (the Pension Equity Act of 1984). The Congressional Budget Office (CBO) has explored the possibility of using a projection of the wage at retirement rather than the wage at termination in calculating the pension benefit (CBO 1987). These initiatives, and other, more sweeping, recommendations, such as those of the President's Commission on Pension Policy (1981), were partly motivated by a concern about the effects of turnover and backloading on pension benefits received at retirement.

Data Sources and Organization of Study

The empirical work in this book uses three major data sources: retrospective data for a five-year period from the 1983 Survey of Consumer Finances (SCF), the 1984-85 Survey of Income and Program Participation (SIPP), and the Panel Study of Income Dynamics (PSID), covering the period 1984 through 1989. All three surveys provide useful information for analyzing the pension-mobility relationship, but the data do have some limitations. The reason for job change is routinely collected only in the PSID, which is the smallest of the samples we have available. In the other surveys, either the reason for job change is not reported or it is available only for a limited, and, as it turns out, highly unrepresentative sample. As a result, much of our empirical work pools layoffs and quits, rather than allowing us to examine layoffs and quits separately.[13] On the other hand, employer-provided information detailing the pension characteristics and formulas is only available for the SCF.[14] Consequently, calculating the extent of backloading using the SIPP and the PSID data requires imputation, by matching pensions to individuals on the basis of personal and job characteristics.

We should note that, throughout the book, all empirical work pertains to men who are initially in their thirties and forties. Prime-aged workers are selected to avoid contaminating the results with retirement-related behavior and to eliminate any mobility associated with school-work choices or with the initial period of job shopping. Analyzing job mobility for women is considerably more complicated than it is for men, since it is much more reasonable to assume in the case of men that participation is constant and that work hours are full time. Our empirical model is not adequate to analyze jointly labor force participation, labor force hours, and mobility decisions, and, as such, would be inappropriate to use in analyzing the mobility decisions of women.

The book is organized as follows. Chapter 2 presents the basic arithmetic of pension backloading. The literature exploring the relationship of pensions to mobility is discussed in chapter 3. Chapter 4 reviews the relevant descriptive statistics and basic multivariate relationships from the three surveys used in this study: the SCF, the PSID, and the SIPP. An econometric model of mobility decisions is developed in chapter 5. Using data from each of the three surveys, an empirical version of the model is estimated in chapter 6. In this model, mobility is a function of the compensation differential between the current and the next best job. The results of these estimations are then used to simulate the effects of pension backloading and of compensation differentials. Chapter 7 provides a reestimation of the model with panel data from the SIPP and the PSID, allowing pension backloading and the remaining compensation premium to have separate and possibly different effects on mobility.[15] The findings in this chapter represent a specification check. Chapter 8 presents the potential policy issues that arise from this work, and our conclusions are discussed in chapter 9.

NOTES

1. These plans, which are called defined benefit plans, base pension eligibility and the yearly pension entitlement on years of service and history of pay on the job. The other major plan type, defined contribution, bases benefits at retirement on the amount accumulated in an account held in the name of the covered worker, with accumulation based on contributions made by the worker and the employer, and on the returns to the investments held by the plan. Defined benefit plans are declining in importance, but they still are the predominant type of primary plan. Often, defined benefit plans are supplemented by defined contribution plans. In recent years, they have been supplemented by a particular type of defined contribution plan, the 401(k) plan. For recent figures on plan coverage by type, see Beller and Lawrence (1992). For discussions of the reasons for these trends, see Clark and McDermed (1990), Gustman and Steinmeier (1992a), Ippolito (forthcoming a), and Kruse (forthcoming a and b).

2. It is possible to design defined contribution plans so that they are backloaded. Examples of such plans abound (Turner 1993). Backloading is attained in higher education, for example, by combining defined contribution plans with special early retirement incentives (Gustman and Steinmeier 1991 and 1992b).   However, as evidence from a representative cross section of the population will show, the degree of backloading in defined contribution plans is very mild because early retirement incentives and other backloading devices are not nearly as common in defined contribution plans as they are in defined benefit plans. Moreover, even when such provisions are present, the size of the incentives they create, and thus their effects on retirement, are modest.

3. The concept of pension capital loss is discussed by Ippolito (1986), by Allen, Clark, and McDermed (1993), and by other students of the pension-mobility relationship. We will return to the question of measuring the pension loss from mobility.

4. More generally, pensions are said to have been promoted by efforts to save at tax-favored rates of return and to meet other goals of covered workers and their employers. For a review of the pension literature, see Gustman, Mitchell, and Steinmeier (1994).

5. The 1993 Allen, Clark, and McDermed article is an important contribution to the literature on pensions and mobility. This study is based on a series of working papers, including Allen, Clark, and McDermed (1991). Certain calculations are only available in the working papers. When appropriate, the working papers will be referenced directly instead of the article.

6. A basic lesson learned from human capital models early on is that human capital investment expenditures should be undertaken as soon as possible (Ben Porath 1967). Although we are aware that much of training costs and all hiring costs occur up front, specific training is distributed throughout the period of worker attachment on the job. For recent data separately reporting training activity at the time of hire and training activity during the course of employment, see U.S. Department of Labor, Bureau of Labor Statistics (1992). For a preliminary effort to relate these data to pension coverage, see Dorsey, Cornwell, and Macpherson (1994).

7. This finding has been confirmed in work by Even and Macpherson (1992). They suggest that failure to vest the employers' contribution in the first few years of employment may discourage mobility of those covered by a defined contribution plan until vesting is attained. This point is of relevance only for a relatively short span of time and cannot account for defined benefit and defined contribution plans having similar, negative effects on turnover for workers throughout their prime working age.

8. Consistent with a view that pensions are used to reduce turnover is a finding that the negative pension-mobility relationship is observed in large firms, which commonly offer defined benefit plans, but not in small firms, which more often offer defined contribution plans (Even and Macpherson 1992). There remains the possibility, however, that other unmeasured characteristics of large and small firm employment may account for this result.

9. The coefficient of pensions in her probit equation for mobility was 0.700, while the coefficient of log wages was 0.608. Both coefficients are highly significant.

10. One might argue that on jobs where a worker's compensation is higher than in the next best opportunity, turnover should be greater because the firm will be encouraged to lay off employees. The evidence is not consistent with this view. We find that where the compensation premium is higher, turnover is lower. Moreover, pension-covered jobs are associated with payment of a compensation premium, yet Mitchell (1982) and Allen, Clark, and McDermed (1993), find that layoffs are lower on pension-covered jobs.

11. Allen, Clark, and McDermed (1993) explain the effect of pensions on mobility through layoffs as a reflection of the firm's commitment to an implicit contract. In such a contract, compensation is deferred. It is argued that laying off workers who have backloaded pensions would violate the implicit contract. We are sympathetic to the idea of an implicit pension contract. There is no other way to explain the *ad hoc* postretirement pension increases that have been granted to most recipients of defined benefit pension plans. Evidence supporting the existence of such increases is contained in Allen, Clark, and Sumner (1986), and in Allen, Clark, and McDermed (1992). Indeed, examination of data from the Panel Study of Income Dynamics (PSID) suggests that cost-of-living adjustments may offset almost half of the adverse effect of inflation on the real value of pensions for those retired on a fixed nominal pension (Gustman and Steinmeier 1993a). Nevertheless, if pension backloading decreases mobility by reducing layoffs, as Allen, Clark, and McDermed find, the question arises as to why firms concerned about mobility would bother to adopt backloaded pensions, since they can control layoffs directly.

12. There is a separate set of concerns about equity. It is argued that, because of pension backloading, those in the population with the least stable job histories, including women and minorities, will have inadequate retirement incomes. For relevant discussions and evidence, see Turner (1993).

13. In the PSID, which is the one survey where quits and layoffs can be readily distinguished, the qualitative results are the same whether the analysis uses quits only or quits and layoffs combined.

14. We use retrospective data from the SCF because, for reasons we discuss, attrition from the 1983-86 SCF panel is systematic and renders the data highly suspect for use in a mobility study. The 1983-89 SCF panel was unavailable at the time this work was done.

15. Censoring of the retrospective data in the SCF prevents estimation of the expanded model with those data.

2

The Basic Arithmetic
of Pension Backloading

Does pension backloading discourage individuals from leaving jobs? This chapter explores the mechanics of pension backloading and evaluates the argument that it provides a severe disincentive to those who would leave pension-covered jobs, especially in the early years of employment.

How large is the effect of backloading on the pension received by an early leaver compared to a worker who remains until qualifying for retirement benefits? Assume, for example, that the worker joins the firm this year at age 30. Further suppose that each year of work results in an increase in the yearly pension that is 1 percent of the salary in the last year of employment. If the worker stays with the firm until qualifying for normal retirement benefits, which in this example occurs at age 62, then the total yearly pension will be equal to 32 percent of final pay. Alternatively, if the worker joins this year at age 30 and leaves at age 40, the pension is calculated as 1 percent of the average salary at age 40 times 10 years of service. However, the pension payments do not begin until the worker reaches retirement age. Accordingly, in this example workers who leave after 10 years of service must wait 22 years before they can receive a pension. Yet the salary used in the computation is fixed in nominal terms, at the level paid 22 years earlier. At 5 percent annual wage growth, the final salary at age 62 is roughly three times the salary at age 40. This early leaver not only receives a lower pension because of having accumulated just one-third of the years of service of the normal retiree, but each year of service is multiplied by a salary level that is roughly one-third of the salary the worker would have received had that individual stayed to retirement age. Accordingly, in this example, an early leaver with the same starting salary and one-third the time at work for a normal retiree would receive a pension of about one-ninth the value of the pension received by the normal retiree. This example indicates the potential effect of backloading on the value of the pension to early versus normal leavers from pension-covered jobs.

Moreover, defined benefit pensions typically provide an additional reward to anyone who remains with the firm until qualifying for early retirement benefits. The additional reward may result from a variety of plan provisions. For example, in the years until they qualify for actual payments from social security, early retirees who are not yet age 62 or 65 may have their pension plan benefits increased by an amount equal to what their future social security benefits will be. Alternatively, the firm may use a reduction in yearly benefits that is smaller than actuarially fair for those who stay until qualifying for early retirement but use an actuarially fair reduction for those vested workers who leave earlier. For example, if the departing employee has not yet qualified for early retirement benefits, the firm may reduce benefits by 6 percent for each year the individual leaves before normal retirement age. For those who have qualified for early retirement, the reduction in the yearly benefit may be 3 percent for each year of retirement before normal retirement age. Under a third mechanism, the generosity of the plan is increased after the employee has been on the job for a specified number of years. For example, the benefit may be equal to 1 percent of the final salary for each of the first 20 years of work, and 2 percent of the final salary for each year of work after that. This type of explicit backloading of the pension formula is limited to some extent by specific provisions of the Employee Retirement Income Security Act of 1974 (ERISA).

Pensions might also reduce turnover via their vesting provisions, which deter workers from leaving firms until they have worked long enough to be guaranteed an eventual retirement benefit (Schiller and Weiss 1979). However, the Tax Reform Act of 1986 specifies that vesting must now occur within a few years of hire, five years if there is cliff vesting and seven years if vesting is graded. This has severely limited the ability of firms to use vesting to reduce turnover of middle-aged workers.

The next section explores the fundamental arithmetic of pension accrual and pension backloading and applies the basic concepts in a series of examples. Then, a measure of pension backloading is developed for use in our later statistical analysis. This measure indicates that backloading can have only a very small effect on the mobility decisions of young workers. The third section presents statistics from a nationally representative sample with matched employer-provided pension plan descriptions. These data indicate the size and variation of pension backloading both from the basic formulas that have been adopted by firms and from the special early retirement benefits offered. The penalty associated with mobility and the increase in compensation for a new job required to offset the pension loss from moving are calculated. Pension accrual is found to be very small within the first decade of employment, and the penalty to mobility created by backloaded pensions is found to be very low for workers who are more than a decade from retiring. In the appendix to this chapter, alternative measures of the potential costs of early mobility are described, analyzed, and compared to the measure that we developed in the chapter. We find our measure equivalent to ones used by Ippolito (1987) and by Lazear and Moore (1988).

Pension Accrual From Defined Benefit Plans

We begin by discussing the arithmetic of pension accrual under defined benefit plans.[1] For purposes of discussion, the simplest type of defined benefit formula, where the yearly benefit in retirement, B_{db}, is given by the product of the generosity parameter a, typically 1 to 2 percentage points, times a measure of the final wage W_f, times the number of years of tenure (service) at retirement T:

$$(2.1) \qquad B_{db} = a W_f T.$$

Assume that wages grow from W_0 in period 0 at a rate of g. Years of service are measured as the difference between the date of separation k and the date of hire j. Under these circumstances, tenure can be expressed as $T = k - j$, and the final wage can be expressed as $W_f = W_0 e^{kg}$, where again W_0 is the wage in period 0.

The total retirement benefit due to work, from hire in year j through any time k, evaluated at time k, is then the present value of the benefit to be paid throughout the retirement years, from date of retirement R to date of death D, taken back to the date k. The further k is from the date of retirement R, the greater the effect of discounting, and the lower the present value of the accruing pension, $P_{db}(k)$. This relationship is given in equation (2.2).[2]

$$(2.2) \quad P_{db}(k) = aW_0 e^{kg}(k-j) e^{-r(R-k)}[1 - e^{-r(D-R)}]/r.$$

The term a is the generosity parameter. The next term is the benefit amount from equation (2.1). The final terms are the result of discounting the benefits received throughout the retirement period at an interest rate r to bring them back to date R, and then further discounting the benefits from the date of retirement to date k. Equation (2.2) holds for $k < R$, that is, for an individual who is working but has not yet qualified for retirement benefits.

To give perspective on the orders of magnitude, we will develop and follow a single example throughout the discussion. We will begin with the relationship between the yearly pension benefit and the present value of the payments made throughout the retirement period. Assuming for purposes of this example that retirement is at age 62 and death is at age 80, the yearly benefits would be received for 18 years. At an interest rate of 8 percent, the present value of the 18 years of benefits on the first day of retirement is about 9.5 times the yearly benefit. (For comparison, at a 6 percent interest rate, the present value of the benefit is worth about 11 times the yearly benefit, whereas if the interest rate is 10 percent, the present value is worth about 8.3 times the yearly benefit.)

Consider now the earnings from work between periods k and $k+1$. They include the wage plus the increase in the value of the pension, less that part of the increase which is due to accruing interest. This amount is the wage plus $P_{db}(k+1) - (1+r)P_{db}(k)$. Following Bulow (1982), the value of the increment in the present value of the pension from remaining employed can be obtained by differentiating equation (2.2) with respect to k and subtracting out $rP_{db}(k)$. Thus equation (2.3) indicates, for any time k preceding the year of eligibility for normal retirement, the path of the marginal increment to pension wealth with additional service:

$$(2.3) \quad \frac{dP_{db}(k)}{dk} - rP_{db}(k) = P_{db}(k)\left[g + \frac{1}{k-j}\right].$$

With positive wage growth and interest rate, the slope of the curve relating the present value of the pension to the date k is positive. Pension accrual from the growth in the wage and from increasing service are reflected in g and $1/(k-j)$ respectively.

Pension backloading is reflected in the fact that before the individual qualifies for retirement, the present value of the pension increases non-linearly with service, with greater proportionate increases for additional service the longer the individual remains on the job. Thus the slope of the function relating the present value of the pension to the date of separation, called the pension accrual rate, is increasing with k.[3] It can also be shown that the pension accrual rate declines sharply after the age of normal retirement.[4]

To illustrate these relationships, we insert assumed values in equations (2.1), (2.2), and (2.3). In particular, we assume the following values for the parameters: $a = 0.01$, $W_{25} = \$20,000$, $g = 0.05$, $r = 0.08$, $j = 25$, $k = 26, 27, ..., 62$, $R = 62$, $D = 80$. Thus, the example pertains to an individual with an initial wage of $20,000 when he or she is hired at age 25, who faces a normal retirement age of 62, and dies with certainty at 80.

Table 2.1 presents the earnings and pension values that result from this example. It illustrates the magnitudes of measures that will be of central concern to us in attempting to determine the way in which pensions affect the incentives for mobility.

Column 2 of table 2.1 reports representative annual earnings during the 37 years of employment, beginning at the individual's 25th birthday, and lasting until retirement at age 62. Column 3 reports the yearly pension benefit starting at age 62, based on the assumption that employment is terminated in the indicated year. Thus, if the individual stays for 37 years, the pension is $47,063 for each year of retirement.

The presence of backloading can be seen in column 4, with a ratio showing the annual benefit if employment were terminated in the indicated year, divided by the benefit if employment were terminated only upon qualifying for normal retirement. Thus, if one stays five years, thereby working 13.5 percent of a full career (5/37), the yearly benefit would be only 2.7 percent of that received had the individual stayed until normal retirement. At the other end of the life cycle, the last two years of work before normal retirement, representing 5 percent of the full period of attachment (2/37), results in an increase of over 14 percent in the yearly pension.

18

Table 2.1 Pensions and the Reward to Work: An Example

(1) Age at separation [k]	(2) Earnings at age k [W_f]	(3) Nominal yearly benefits at age 62 [B_k]	(4) Ratio of yearly benefits to potential benefits [B_k / B_{62}]	(5) Total pension [$P_{db}(k)$]	(6) Pension benefit accrual rate [$dP_{db}(k)/dk$]	(7) Ratio of accrual to compensation (excluding interest rate effect)
26	$ 21,025	$ 210	0.004	$ 113	$ 127	0.006
30	25,681	1,284	0.027	947	312	0.009
35	32,974	3,297	0.070	3,627	834	0.016
40	42,340	6,351	0.135	10,422	2,050	0.028
45	54,366	10,873	0.231	26,619	4,791	0.047
50	69,807	17,452	0.371	63,737	10,835	0.076
55	89,634	26,890	0.571	146,508	23,930	0.120
60	115,092	40,282	0.856	327,418	51,919	0.183
62	127,196	47,063	1.000	448,903	70,490	0.214

NOTE: This example is based on equations (2.1), (2.2) and (2.3) and assumes $a = 0.01$, $W_{25} = \$20,000$, $g = 0.05$, $r = 0.08$, $j = 25$, $k = 26, 27, ..., 62$, $R = 62$, and $D = 80$.

Because of pension backloading, the worker who stays until retirement age will enjoy a rapidly accruing pension. Column 6 shows the pension accrual including the interest. Column 7 computes the ratio of the accrual to total compensation (wages plus accrual, which is column 2 plus column 6). However, in calculating the pension accrual, the interest term is omitted as in equation (2.3); this isolates the effects of working another year on the wage and service used in computing benefits and eliminates the change in the present value of the pension brought about when the base period advances one year. The figures in column 7 show that the value of the pension accrual rises rapidly. After 20 years of attachment, it will reach 5 percent of compensation.

Column 7 shows that, although the pension accrual represents only about half of one percent of compensation in the first year of employment, it is almost a fifth of compensation as the individual comes within two years of qualifying for normal retirement. Even a basic defined benefit plan, with a generosity coefficient of only 1 percent, provides the worker with the opportunity to increase compensation by amounts that appear to be substantial.

Special early retirement benefits create additional incentives for the worker to stay with the firm. Further, many defined benefit pension plans base benefits on two or three formulas. One formula may pertain to benefits for those who leave the firm before qualifying for early retirement (i.e., for terminated-vested employees), and another to those who qualify for normal retirement, with various treatments for work past normal retirement date. There may also be another formula, or perhaps an adjustment factor applied to the formula for normal retirement benefits, to determine benefits for those who qualify for early retirement. Special temporary benefits at early retirement, such as the adjustment until social security eligibility and the granting of additional years to credited service, would create a "spike" in the pension accrual profile at the early retirement age.

In addition to the discontinuous benefit accrual at early retirement, pension wealth may change dramatically at other dates. For instance, some plans specify generous benefits for workers until they reach a prespecified level of service, while drastically reducing accruals for work after that point. In general, defined benefit plans are not actuarially neutral with regard to retirement ages, paying wealth values that differ substantially, depending on when the worker leaves.

A Measure of Pension Loss From Mobility

Our literature review in chapter 3 shows that a number of authors have attributed an important part of the negative relationship between pension coverage and mobility to the effects of backloading of defined benefit pension plans. Consequently, the mobility equations we estimate will be used to isolate the effect of pension backloading. It follows that we should develop a measure of pension backloading and explore its importance in compensation.

The measure of pension backloading we will employ compares pension accrual in the defined benefit plan with pension accrual in a comparable defined contribution plan, i.e, having the same value at retirement. Backloading is simply the difference between the present value of the defined contribution plan and the defined benefit plan. Although it might at first appear that the definition of pension capital loss that we use is rather specialized, the appendix to this chapter will show that it is equivalent to the measures that are commonly used in the literature.

Consider first the change in value of a defined contribution pension with additional service. For the case in which the rate of growth of wages, g, is unequal to the interest rate, r, the value of a defined contribution plan with contribution rate c, as of year k, or $P_{dc}(k)$, for an individual hired in year j, is[5]

$$(2.4) \qquad P_{dc}(k) = \frac{c}{g-r} W_0 e^{gk} [1 - e^{(r-g)(k-j)}] \, .$$

If g is equal to r, the value of the defined contribution plan is equal to[6]

$$P_{dc}(k) = c W_0 e^{rk} (k - j) \, .$$

In the case where the wage growth rate and interest rate are equal, the balance in the pension plan is simply the amount deposited in year k, which is fraction c of the wage, times the number of years of service. Deposits made in earlier years will grow at the rate r due to compounding and will just keep up with the increase in the value of the contribution to the pension, which is rising due to wage growth.

The slope of the profile is given by

$$(2.5) \qquad \frac{dP_{dc}(k)}{dk} - rP_{dc}(k) = \frac{c}{g-r} W_0 e^{gk} [g-1]$$

for g not equal to r. For g equal to r, the slope is

$$\frac{dP_{dc}(k)}{dk} - rP_{dc}(k) = cW_0 e^{rk}$$

$$= P_{dc}(k) \left[\frac{1}{k-j}\right].$$

Notice that when $g = r$, the proportionate change in the value of the pension with increasing service is equal to the proportionate change in service ($1/(k-j)$). In addition, the pension value grows with r. This simply reflects the fact that the nominal value of the deposit is adjusted in accordance with the interest rate for different base periods.[7]

To compare the loss from mobility under a defined benefit and a *comparable* defined contribution plan, it is necessary to discuss what we mean by comparability. A defined contribution and defined benefit plan are said to be comparable if they generate the same present value at the retirement age specified by the defined benefit plan. Equating the right-hand sides of equations (2.2) and (2.4) and setting $k = R$, equation (2.6) solves for the generosity coefficient of the comparable defined contribution plan, $c*$, which is

$$(2.6) \qquad c* = \frac{a(R-j)[1 - e^{-r(D-R)}]/r}{\frac{1}{g-r}[1 - e^{(r-g)(R-j)}]}$$

if r is different from g, or

$$c* = a[1 - e^{-r(D-R)}]/r$$

if $r = g$.

As noted, a convenient measure of the disincentive to mobility at year k created by a pension is the present value of the comparable defined contribution plan evaluated at time k minus the present value of the defined benefit plan at time k.

$$(2.7) \qquad \text{Backloading} = P_{dc}(k) - P_{db}(k).$$

To illustrate the orders of magnitude involved, and the path over time of the disincentive to mobility created by pension backloading, table 2.2 continues the example developed in table 2.1. This example indicates the effect of backloading under the assumption that the plan is a simple defined benefit plan with no special benefits at early retirement and does not use different formulas for those who qualify for early or normal retirement. Comparable measures of backloading for a nationally representative sample, with plans that most often do include these features, are presented in the following discussion. Table 2.2 allows us to focus on the size of the effects of backloading that is a result of the basic defined benefit formula. Generosity coefficients that exceed 1 percent would lead to upward adjustments in the figures in the table, while the presence of social security or other offsets would require downward adjustments.

Column 2 calculates the increase in the present value (discounted to year k) of the defined benefit plan between age k and age 62, the retirement age in the plan. This amount is the value of the pension if the individual stays until the retirement age, discounted back to year k, less the value if the individual were to quit working at the firm after year k. Column 3 makes the corresponding calculation for the defined contribution plan.

Backloading, or pension capital loss, is the difference between these two columns, as illustrated in column 4. Since the contribution percentage for the defined contribution plan is chosen so that the two plans have equal value at retirement, $P_{db}(R) = P_{dc}(R)$, the backloading amount simplifies to $P_{dc}(k) - P_{db}(k)$. Notice that pension capital loss takes on an inverse U shape when it is related to tenure. According to related examples in Petersen (1992), these patterns are also typical of other plan formulas beside the basic, final-average-salary defined benefit plan.

The importance of backloading relative to the value of the future pension accruals and relative to future compensation is indicated in columns 5 and 6, respectively. The numbers in column 6 may be interpreted as the wage increase that would be required to just offset the pension capital loss that would occur if a worker changed jobs (assuming that both jobs had the same kind of pension).

These numbers show that backloading can have only a very small effect on the mobility decisions of young workers. For those in their

Table 2.2 Pension Backloading: An Example

(1) Separation age [k]	(2) Future increase in present value of db plan $[P_{db}(R)\,e^{-r(R-k)}$ $- P_{db}(k)]$	(3) Future increase in present value of dc plan $[P_{dc}(R)\,e^{-r(R-k)}$ $- P_{dc}(k)]$	(4) Backloading $[P_{dc}(k) - P_{db}(k)]$	(5) Ratio of backloading to future increase in present value of db plan	(6) Ratio of backloading to present value of future compensation
26	$ 25,086	$24,088	$ 998	.040	.008
30	33,756	27,492	6,263	.186	.011
35	48,143	31,756	16,386	.340	.025
40	66,809	35,488	31,321	.469	.042
45	88,597	37,679	50,918	.575	.063
50	108,145	36,612	71,533	.661	.088
55	109,909	29,454	80,455	.732	.119
60	55,112	11,627	43,485	.789	.156
62	0	0	0	-	-

NOTE: This example is based on equationS (2.1), (2.2) and (2.3) and assumes $a = 0.01$, $W_0 = \$20,000$, $g = 0.05$, $r = 0.08$, $j = 25$, $k = 26, 27, ..., 62$, $R = 62$, and $D = 80$.

first decade of employment, pension capital loss is minor and is easily overcome by a modest raise on the new job. Even for an individual who is 45 years old and has 20 years of experience, the required raise is only 6.3 percent. Of course, as the retirement age is reduced, or as the worker ages, the disincentive for mobility increases. Plans that are more generous relative to the wage will have stronger effects. However, these figures strongly suggest that pension backloading will constitute a noticeable fraction of compensation only for those within a decade or so of qualifying for early or normal retirement benefits.

The foregoing examples set the stage for an examination of disincentives to mobility in actual pension data. Such data will take into account the wide variation in the features of pension benefit formulas, the differences in requirements for early and normal retirement, and the various special changes that often take place in pension plans at the time that individuals qualify for early or normal retirement. These factors raise the penalty for leaving a firm once an individual is covered by a defined benefit pension plan. Accordingly, we now turn to measures of pension backloading based on the pensions held by a representative sample of the population.

Pension Accrual and Disincentives to Mobility

To this point, we have considered a numerical example of the disincentive effects for mobility created by the backloading of defined benefit plans. The disincentive effects result from the use of the standard final average salary formula. As previously noted, pension plans also discourage mobility by providing additional special benefits only to those who stay until qualifying for early or normal retirement.

In actual data on pension plans, there is wide variation in the formulas, in the ages of eligibility for early and normal benefits, and in the special benefits. It is therefore useful to examine the pension accrual profiles and related mobility incentives for a representative sample of the population.

At the date of writing, there was only one population survey—the 1983 Survey of Consumer Finances (SCF)—that provided detailed, employer-supplied, descriptions of pension benefit formulas and earnings histories. All of the statistical analysis of the pension-mobility relationship in this book will make use of the pension provider information from the 1983 SCF. Specifically, the SCF information will be used to determine the incentives for mobility that are facing workers in pension-covered jobs.

Table 2.3 summarizes the pension accrual profiles that would be experienced by the population of male pension-covered workers in the 1983 SCF. To understand the variability in the plans, the figures in the table suppose that all workers were hired at age 25. The table illustrates the average incentives and the variability of incentives at different ages. The patterns in the table would be similar for workers hired at other ages, although the exact figures would vary.

To obtain the results presented in the table, we considered a sample of pension-covered individuals. We used the individual's reported current wage and projected this wage forward and backward over time on the basis of the experience and tenure coefficients from a standard wage equation. This wage stream was then matched to pensions in the 1983 SCF on the basis of industry, occupation, firm size, union status, and wage level.[8] The wage stream is applied to these pension plans to calculate the path of accumulation of pension rights.[9] In these calculations it is assumed that any nominal amounts in the plans are adjusted upward with the general level of wages. Post-retirement benefits are increased by 38 percent of the inflation rate, conforming to results found in Allen, Clark, and Sumner (1986).[10] The results are weighted and aggregated to form the results reported in the table.

The first block of results in the table indicates the ratio of the value of discounted accumulated pension benefits (pension wealth) to the value of discounted cumulative wages (wage wealth) for individuals (all presumed hired at age 25) who have reached various ages. The middle column of data indicates the median ratios, and the first and third columns provide the first and third quartiles as measures of variability. As expected, all ratios grow at an increasing rate up to about age 55, after which the growth rate declines and they flatten out or decline slightly. It is interesting to consider the variability of the ratios. At age 55 the value for the third quartile (13.5 percent) is over two and a half times the value for the first quartile (5.2 percent). At age 65, by which time everyone in the sample should be eligible to collect full normal retirement benefits, the third quartile value is almost twice the first quartile value.

Table 2.3 Pension Accruals and Wealth for Defined Benefit Plans from the 1983 Survey of Consumer Finances (Assuming Age of Hire is 25)

	First quartile	Median	Third quartile
By age:	**Pension wealth / wage wealth**		
35	1.1%	1.7%	3.1%
40	1.6	2.5	4.2
45	2.1	3.4	5.7
50	3.1	5.1	8.7
55	5.2	9.1	13.5
60	6.2	9.5	12.7
65	5.4	8.7	10.5
By age:	**Pension accrual / annual wage**		
35	1.6%	2.6%	5.8%
40	2.5	4.3	7.0
45	3.9	6.7	10.6
50	6.2	10.3	16.8
55	-1.0	5.9	15.3
60	-9.8	.7	9.7
65	-36.8	-20.6	-10.5
Relative to plan retirement ages:			
Pre-retirement	6.4	11.1	17.5
For those with early retirement			
Spike at early retirement age	13.3	26.8	114.9
Early retirement to normal retirement	3.3	10.5	18.2
Spike at normal retirement age	-2.1	8.0	20.6
For those without early retirement			
Spike at normal retirement age	106.5	190.9	229.2
Post-retirement	-22.0	-10.3	-5.3
	Plan retirement ages		
Early retirement age	55	55	55
Normal retirement age	60	62	65

The second block of results in table 2.3 measures the pension accrual rate, or the ratio of the annual change in pension wealth to the annual change in wage wealth. The numerator of these ratios is simply the increase in the expected value of the pension due to working another year, excluding that part of the increase attributable to interest and to having survived the year. Future values are multiplied by survival probabilities, which increase at a given future age as the individual lives longer. The denominator is the wage that is received from working that year. Negative entries reflect the situation in which the value of the pension is actually lowered by working another year, principally because the worker is already eligible for benefits and will give up a year's benefits if he or she keeps working. In the table, the median plan reaches a peak at age 50, when pension accruals reach 10.3 percent of wages. At age 55, accruals in the median plan drop to 5.9 percent of wages that year. Age 55 is when a worker hired at age 25 will have achieved 30 years of experience at the firm, and many plans offer either full normal retirement benefits or early retirement benefits for workers who reach age 55 or who have 30 years of service.

In all quartiles, the marginal pension incentives to remain at a firm rise very rapidly up to age 50, which is before most individuals are eligible for early retirement benefits. After individuals become eligible for early retirement benefits, the marginal incentives drop up to age 65 almost as rapidly as they previously rose. At age 65 and thereafter, when all individuals are eligible for full normal retirement benefits, the marginal incentives drop precipitously. Again, the plans exhibit a great deal of variation in their incentives. At age 45 and earlier, the third quartile value is almost three times the first quartile value, and after that the variability is even more striking. By age 60 the bottom quarter of the plans are significantly penalizing employees for further work, while the top quarter are rewarding employees almost as much as ever.

The third block of results in table 2.3 highlights evidence of discrete jumps in pension values at the ages of early and/or normal retirement, similar to findings reported by Kotlikoff and Wise (1987a). The "spikes" in the table refer to the increase in pension value, relative to wages, that occurs in the year the individual first reaches eligibility for early or normal retirement benefits. Preretirement refers to the three years immediately prior to the early retirement spike year (or normal retirement spike year, if the plan does not provide for early retirement).

The row labeled "early retirement to normal retirement" refers to the years immediately before the normal retirement spike year but after eligibility for early retirement; postretirement refers to the three years immediately following the normal retirement spike year.[11] For example, in the year of work that results in eligibility for early retirement, the value of the median pension jumps by an amount equal to 26.8 percent of the wage earned in that year.

The table shows that the majority of plans yield a substantial increment in pension value upon eligibility for early retirement, with the median equal to 26.8 percent of the annual wage. In many cases these gains are enormous. For a quarter of all plans, the increase in pension value exceeds the value of the wage in the year of early retirement eligibility. Moreover, among plans that do not provide for early retirement, the spikes at normal retirement are very large and highly variable. The first quartile shows an increase in pension value that is a little bit larger than the wage in the year of normal retirement; for the third quartile, the increase in pension value is more than double the value of the wage.

The final two rows of the table report the early and normal retirement ages found in these plans. For a majority of the plans, including the first and third quartiles, eligibility for early retirement benefits begins at age 55 for an individual hired at age 25. There is somewhat more variation in the age of eligibility for normal retirement benefits, with the median at 62 and the first and third quartiles at 60 and 65, respectively.

Table 2.4 gives pension values for defined contribution plans in the 1983 SCF.[12] There is little evidence that defined contribution plans are sufficiently backloaded to create major disincentives to mobility. While defined contribution plans can theoretically be backloaded (Turner 1993), in practice backloading of defined contribution plans does not appear to be severe.

The calculations underlying table 2.3 clearly indicate that defined benefit pension plans may provide substantial rewards to continued work in the years just before the early retirement age. Moreover, even standardizing completely for the date of hire, the incentives vary considerably among the plans. This is especially true of the spikes, which provide particularly strong and variable incentives for retirement not captured in any currently available household-based data set except the

SCF.[13] In addition to affecting retirement decisions, the large accruals in the years just before early retirement may also affect mobility at previous ages; an individual who leaves the firm early for any reason gives up the opportunity to earn these accruals. The question is whether the magnitude of this incentive is enough to deter mid-career and younger workers from moving.

Table 2.4 Pension Accruals and Wealth for Defined Contribution Plans for the 1983 Survey of Consumer Finances (Assuming Age of Hire is 25)

	First quartile	Median	Third quartile
By age:	Pension wealth / wage wealth		
35	7.8%	8.8%	14.5%
40	8.7	9.7	15.0
45	8.7	10.5	15.1
50	8.7	10.5	15.2
55	8.7	10.6	15.5
60	8.7	10.6	15.4
65	8.7	10.6	15.6
By age:	Pension accrual / annual wage		
35	12.4%	13.1%	17.6%
40	8.7	13.1	17.0
45	8.7	10.9	15.4
50	8.7	10.9	15.3
55	8.7	10.9	15.3
60	8.7	10.9	15.3
65	8.7	10.6	15.3

To answer this question, we calculated the size of the disincentives to mobility created by pension backloading for the sample of 31- to 50-year-olds in the SCF in 1978. This is the base period we will use for mobility analysis using the SCF data. The examples analyzed in the second section of this chapter suggested that there is a very small disincentive to mobility for individuals in this age range created by the backloading of the basic pension formula. The following discussion shows that this result is also reflected in the actual data from a representative population sample, even when special early retirement benefits are included.

Table 2.5 attempts to decompose the 1978 average job compensation into primary components due to the wage, to the pension benefit under an equivalent defined contribution plan, and pension backloading.[14] This table examines pension capital loss, including the effects of special benefits for those who stay until qualifying for early retirement, calculated from the employer Pension Provider Survey of the SCF, which is a nationally representative survey of prime-aged pension-covered workers.

Table 2.5 Decomposition of Average Hourly Compensation Until Retirement for Those with Defined Benefit Plans

	Compensation level	Percent of compensation
Amount due to:		
Wage	$12.58	87.1
Pension without backloading	1.49	10.3
Backloading	.38	2.6
Total	14.45	100.0

SOURCE: Authors' calculations of 1978 base period earnings using the 1983 Survey of Consumer Finances.

Compensation is calculated as the average per hour amount of (discounted) wages plus increases in (discounted) pension values between 1978 and either the individual's expected date of retirement from full-time work or the normal retirement age specified in the individual's pension plan, whichever is earlier. If the individual did not provide an expected retirement age, the terminal date for the compensation calculations is taken to be the normal retirement age in the pension plan. Real wages are imputed on the basis of a wage profile similar to the one used for table 2.3. The rationale for calculating the average compensation between the current date and retirement is as follows. To avoid the pension capital loss and reap the high accruals just before retirement, the worker must remain at the current firm until retirement.

However, the financial incentives to remain with the current firm are not just the pension accruals but also the wages that will be earned over the period.

The first column of data in table 2.5 divides the total hourly compensation until retirement for pension-covered workers into three components: the wage, the value of the pension from working until retirement under an equivalent defined contribution plan, and the value of backloading. The first figure in the column sums up the discounted wages until retirement and divides by the number of hours until retirement. The second figure in the column asks the question: What would the portion of compensation until retirement that is due to the pension have been if the pension amount over the lifetime of the job had been held the same, but the pension value had accumulated in the fashion of a defined contribution plan? Again, the resulting number is divided by the number of hours until retirement. The third figure, pension backloading, is the pension loss that occurs because actual pension plans accumulate value disproportionately at the end of the job rather than smoothly over the life of the job. The backloading total is also divided by the number of hours until retirement. The figures in the table are averages over the samples of pension-covered individuals in the SCF.

The loss amount due to pension backloading, amortized over the time until retirement, is less than 3 percent of compensation. Because the individuals in this sample have over 22 years until retirement, however, the lump-sum value of the loss is still substantial. The typical worker in a pension-covered job would suffer approximately a $17,000 pension loss if the individual were to leave that job. On the other hand, there are over 22 years in which to make up this loss in the new job. At 2,000 hours per year, the new job would have to pay about 38 cents more per hour, or a relatively small raise of about 2.6 percent of compensation, in order to make up for the pension loss. This amortization appears to be the appropriate procedure to use in determining what a new job must pay in order to equal the earnings if the individual were to continue in the present job. The dollar value of the pension loss may look sizable, but it is only a relatively small component of the value of the job. More sizable is the value of the pension itself. Over the life of the job, the nonbackloaded portion of the pension contributes about 10.3 percent of compensation.

The loss amounts do not appear to be very sensitive to the interest rates used to evaluate the losses. To illustrate, consider the worker whose pension is shown in table 2.2. This worker joins the firm at age 25 and plans to retire at 62, which is typical of pension-covered workers in this sample. Recall that the pension pays benefits equal to 1 percent of the final salary times years of service. Assuming an interest rate of 8 percent and a nominal wage growth of 5 percent, the pension capital loss for the worker is equal to 65.6 percent of the annual wage at age 45. Raising both the interest rate and the wage growth rate by 4 percentage points to an interest rate of 12 percent and a nominal wage growth of 9 percent, the capital loss is 69.4 percent of the annual wage at age 45. Evidently the increase in capital loss due to the greater spread between current and retirement wages in the second case is essentially offset by the increased erosion of postretirement benefits due to the nominal nature of those benefits. In both of these examples, the loss would be only about 4 percent of compensation until retirement.

In sum, the data from the Pension Provider Survey attached to the SCF confirm the finding that the spikes in the pension accrual profile are large and variable at the early retirement age. The data also strongly confirm the implications from analyzing pension benefit formulas in the abstract: defined benefit plans do not create large disincentives to mobility from the option value of the pension. For the sample of pensions covering prime-aged workers in the SCF, the cost of mobility to pension-covered workers from the backloading of pension plans amounts to less than 3 percent of compensation. Only a modest raise on the new job is needed to offset the disincentive to mobility created by backloaded pension plans, taking account of the disincentives derived from the backloading of the basic defined benefit formula and from the special benefits offered at early retirement.

Appendix to Chapter 2
Methodology for Calculating Pension Backloading

This appendix compares the measure of backloading developed in chapter 2 with the measures used in leading studies by Ippolito (1986) and Lazear and Moore (1988). It shows that the measure of pension loss from mobility described here is a generalization of "capital loss" measures used in the other studies.

To review, our backloading calculation begins by determining the contribution rate that would be required for a defined contribution plan to achieve the same value as the actual plan at the projected retirement date. Next, the current value of this hypothetical defined contribution plan is calculated, by measuring how much value the actual plan would have accrued were it not backloaded. The difference between this value and the current value of the actual plan is a measure of the backloading loss.

This measure of backloading is equal to Ippolito's calculation of capital loss for the standard defined benefit plan he examines. For the more complicated plans occasionally encountered in the SCF, our generalized measure of capital loss is more appropriate than Ippolito's.

Consider a simple defined benefit plan that calculates benefits by multiplying a generosity factor times years of service times final salary. For such a pension, Ippolito defines capital loss L as the loss in value of the pension if the current wage is used in the formula rather than the wage at retirement, holding years of service at its current value. Using the notation developed earlier in the chapter:

$$(2.8) \qquad L = \int_{R}^{D} a\,(W_R - W_k)\,T_k e^{-r(t-k)}\,dt$$

where a is the generosity factor of the plan, T_k and W_k are tenure and the wage, respectively, at age k, and R is the retirement age.[15]

If wages grow at the same rate as the interest rate, this expression can be manipulated as follows:

$$(2.9) \qquad L = \int_{R}^{D} a W_R T_k e^{-r(t-k)}\,dt - \int_{R}^{D} a W_k T_k e^{-r(t-k)}\,dt$$

$$= \int_{j}^{R} c^* W_t e^{-r(t-k)}\,dt - \int_{R}^{D} a W_k T_k e^{-r(t-k)}\,dt$$

where j is the age at hire. The first term in the last of the equalities in equation (2.9) is the current value of a defined contribution plan with a contribution rate

c^*, and the second term is the present value of the defined benefit pension. Note that c^* satisfies the relationship

$$(2.10) \qquad \int_R^D a W_R T_R e^{-r(t-R)} \, dt = \int_j^R c^* W_t e^{-r(t-R)} \, dt$$

which is to say that the values of the defined benefit and defined contribution plans are equal at age R. This can be algebraically manipulated to yield

$$\int_R^D a W_R T_R e^{-r(t-R)} \, dt = \int_j^R c^* W_R \, dt$$

$$= c^* W_R T_R$$

$$\Rightarrow \int_R^D a W_R T_k e^{-r(t-k)} \, dt = c^* W_R e^{-r(k-R)} T_k$$

$$= c^* W_k T_k$$

$$= \int_j^k c^* W_k \, dt$$

$$= \int_j^k c^* W_t e^{-r(t-k)} \, dt \, .$$

The last line of this condition enables us to move from the first line in equation (2.9) to the bottom line. Since the top line of equation (2.9) is Ippolito's definition of capital loss, and the bottom line is the measure of capital loss used in this study, the two definitions are equal for the type of plan considered by Ippolito.

This approach of comparing the current values of a defined benefit plan with that of a comparably valued (at retirement) defined contribution plan can be extended to more complicated pensions as well. For example, a pension may calculate benefits as equal to 1 percent of final salary times years of service of up to 20 years plus 1.5 percent of final salary times years of service past 20 years. In this kind of pension, simply plugging the wage at retirement into the formula yields an understatement of the extent of backloading. Alternatively, many pensions make a more favorable formula available to individuals who work with the firm until retirement. Again, simply plugging the retirement wage into the currently applicable formula understates backloading for individuals below the retirement age. In both of these cases, comparing the current value of the pension with that of a defined contribution pension reaching the same value at retirement will yield a better measure of the backloading.

The pension values (inclusive of backloading losses) used in this study are also related to the pension "option values" used by Lazear and Moore (1988). Lazear and Moore effectively define the option value of a pension at time k as

$$\frac{P(R^*)}{(1+r)^{R^*-k}} - P(k) \, ,$$

where $P(t)$ is the present value of future benefits should the worker leave at year t, k is the current age, R^* is the retirement age that maximizes the preceding expression, and r is the discount rate. The option value is simply the difference between the pension value at the optimal retirement age, discounted back to the current age, and its current value. It is important because the value of many pensions jumps a sizable amount when eligibility for early retirement is reached and because part of the value of current employment is the opportunity to continue working and to realize this increment in pension value. Calculated at the same age of retirement, the option value is the equivalent to the pension part of future compensation used in this study.

One difference between our measure of the pension portion of future compensation and the option value may be noted. The measure used here computes the pension as of the age at which the individual intends to retire. The option is often calculated at the age at which $P(t)$ is maximized in value. The advantage of using the intended age of retirement in calculating the worth of the pension is that the option has value only to the extent that the individual intends to exercise it.

NOTES

1. The following discussion incorporates material from Gustman and Steinmeier (1989a). A number of the basic relationships discussed here have been analyzed by Barnow and Ehrenberg (1979), Bulow (1981, 1982) and Kotlikoff and Wise (1985, 1987a).

2. To be more specific about the derivation of equation (2.2),

$$P_{db}(k) = \int_R^D aW_f T e^{-r(t-k)} dt$$

$$= \int_R^D aW_0 e^{kg} (k-j) e^{-r(t-k)} dt$$

$$= aW_0 e^{kg} (k-j) e^{-r(R-k)} [1 - e^{-r(D-R)}]/r.$$

Note $e^{-r(t-k)}$ is the product of $e^{-r(t-R)}$ and $e^{-r(R-k)}$.

In the empirical results in the third section and in the remaining chapters, the benefits are multiplied by the probability of living to collect them. However, since none of the theoretical points in this chapter is affected by the existence of uncertainty about the length of life, the formulations use a certain lifespan in order to avoid undue complexity.

3. More specifically, the second derivative of the pension accrual rate with respect to k is positive because wage growth and service growth are interacting. See also Kotlikoff and Wise (1985, 1987a).

4. For $k > R$, benefits commence upon retirement, and the lower limit of the integral in equation (2.2) becomes k instead of R. As a result, the present value of the pension as of year k is

$P_{db}(k) = a W_0 e^{kg} (k-j) [1 - e^{-r(D-k)}]/r.$

For the case where the individual works past normal retirement age, and credit is given for such work, the pension accrual rate is given by

$dP_{db}(k)/dk - rP_{db}(k) = P_{db}(k) \{g + 1/(k-j) - r/[1 - e^{-r(D-k)}]\}.$

In this expression, the last term in the brackets reflects the fact that once the individual qualifies for retirement benefits, benefits are foregone when retirement is postponed. If this loss is sufficiently large, the value of the pension may begin to decline as soon as the normal retirement age is reached. In any case, the relative importance of this loss increases with k. This implies that eventually the value of the pension must begin to decline and will do so at an accelerating rate.

5. The formula simply dates the pension contribution by the employer, which is a fraction c of the wage at time t. It then provides interest from whatever time the pension contribution was made until the time k, when the amount in the pension fund is totaled. Integrating this expression yields the equation in the text.

$$P_{dc}(k) = \int_j^k cW_t e^{-r(t-k)} dt$$

$$= \int_j^k cW_0 e^{gt} e^{-r(t-k)} dt.$$

6. In this case, the formula in the previous footnote simplifies to

$$P_{dc}(k) = \int_{j}^{k} c W_0 e^{-rk} dt \, .$$

7. Note once again that there is no explicit allowance here for the effects of mortality, although these effects are included in the empirical work in the next section and in all subsequent chapters.

8. Experience with the 1989 SCF suggests that the pension wealth and incentive distributions are approximately the same whether pensions are matched on an individual basis or by this procedure.

9. More specifically, real wages each year are imputed on the basis of a regression of log wages on experience, experience squared, tenure, tenure squared, interactions of both experience and tenure with education, union status and firm size, and a set of other standard explanatory variables including dummy variables for marital status, race, sex, health status, union status, whether the firm size exceeded 100 employees, SMSA residence, industry (eight variables), and region (four variables). A wage profile is created by extrapolating the observed wage before and after dates on the basis of the estimated coefficients for the experience and tenure variables in the wage equation. Pension values are calculated by applying the resulting wage profile to the individual's own pension. These calculations assume an interest rate of 6.3 percent, nominal wage growth of 5.1 percent, and an inflation rate of 4.0 percent, roughly corresponding to the Social Security IIB scenario at the time of the observed mobility behavior (Social Security Trustees Annual Report 1988). All compensation amounts are discounted to 1983 and expressed in 1983 dollars.

10. Slightly higher pension adjustments with inflation are found in Gustman and Steinmeier (1993a), but both estimates are relatively close.

11. It should also be noted that these profiles are somewhat different from those that would be observed today. Pension plans must now continue to credit work beyond the normal retirement age. As a result, the negative accrual rates reported at age 65 and for the post-retirement period are considerably more muted.

12. These are plans that did not have any defined benefit component.

13. The message on the variability of pension incentives among plans has been particularly emphasized by Kotlikoff and Wise (1985, 1987a). An implication is that there is a great deal of room for error in studies that match pension incentives on the basis of plan characteristics. Further evidence on this point is provided in Gustman and Steinmeier (1989a), where we examine the relationship of pension incentives to plan characteristics.

14. Comparable results are obtained for pensions in the 1983 base period, that is, for the pensions that will be used to impute the incentives affecting mobility decisions of participants in the SIPP and PSID surveys.

15. Again, the effects of an uncertain lifetime could be introduced by multiplying the benefit amounts times the appropriate survival probabilities. Such a change would have no effect on the points being made in this section, so the simpler notation is used.

3

The Literature Relevant to the Pension-Mobility Relationship

This chapter highlights and discusses results from the literature on pensions and mobility. The first section highlights the findings in the literature, while the second section evaluates these findings. Each section begins with a discussion of the evidence on the penalty to mobile workers created by pension backloading. The discussion next briefly reviews explanations of why firms might value the ability to influence mobility. Third, there is a discussion of reduced form results that indicate a negative association between pension coverage and mobility. Fourth is a review of a more recent effort to relate an explicit measure of pension backloading to mobility. Fifth, some additional findings are discussed. A final section discusses a number of unresolved issues from the literature on wage determination.[1]

Evidence from the Literature

Pension Backloading and Disincentives to Mobility

A fundamental reason why pensions might discourage mobility is that under the defined benefit plan, benefits accrue disproportionately in the later years of employment. As seen in chapter 2, backloading arises because the defined benefit plan bases yearly pension benefits on final earnings and years of covered employment. Both annual earnings and years of covered employment increase with tenure on the job, but when a person leaves the firm, the pay figure used in calculating the pension benefit is frozen. Moreover, there are special benefits for those who stay with the firm until qualifying for early retirement. Consequently, pensions received by terminated, vested workers are disproportionately reduced in value from the pension that would have been received had the worker remained with the firm until qualifying for retirement benefits. The backloading of defined benefit plans makes it more costly to leave a pension covered job.[2] To the extent that pensions increase the cost of moving, they would reduce the likelihood of mobility.

Researchers of pensions have been well aware of the phenomenon of pension backloading. Some relate backloading directly to mobility. Often, however, the discussion of backloading focuses on its ramifications for implicit contracts. A central concern is to determine the extent of the firm's pension liability, or how that liability varies with worker tenure.[3] Studies also focus on the question of pension adequacy in retirement. Backloading reduces pension incomes for workers who have held many jobs. Researchers have also focused on the relationship of mobility to the replacement rate, the ratio of the yearly benefit to the final wage or some average wage (Turner 1993). Those with a strong interest in the determination and adequacy of retirement incomes look primarily at the effect of mobility on pension benefits received, rather than focusing on the effects of pension provisions and backloading on mobility.

It is useful to consider some examples of pension backloading from the literature. For comparison, the pension backloading we calculated in table 2.4 represents a little over $17,000 in 1983 dollars. Since the wage was $12.58 per hour (table 2.5), or about $25,000 for a 2,000-hour year, the backloading represents about 70 percent of a year's wages.

The first example is from Ippolito (1986), who presents an example of pension capital loss from mobility. His illustration is for a worker hired at age 35, with normal retirement at age 65, an annual real wage of $10,000 and a real interest rate of zero (the interest rate equals inflation). Nominal wages are presumed to grow at the same rate as inflation. To simplify the annuity calculation, Ippolito assumes that, with retirement at 65, there is a lump-sum payment of 15 percent of the wage times years of service. Given these assumptions, the data in table 3.1 are generated.

The last two columns report the loss in the pension as a fraction of the yearly wage ($10,000). These losses are a somewhat larger percentage of the wage than are the amortized amounts of pension losses discussed in the paragraphs following table 2.5. There are a number of reasons for these differences. One factor is that a later age of retirement is assumed in Ippolito's example than is apparent in the Survey of Consumer Finances (SCF) data underlying table 2.5. Also, Ippolito assumes a lump-sum settlement of 15 percent of the wage times years of service, so that higher inflation does not erode the pension after the individual retires.[4] In addition, the pension assumed by Ippolito is somewhat more generous than are the pensions found in the SCF.[5] Nevertheless, despite the fact that we are comparing a theoretical example with real data, and that a number of assumptions in Ippolito's example tend to exaggerate pension backloading, the conclusions as to the likely penalty to mobility from pension backloading are of comparable magnitudes.

Table 3.1 An Example of Loss from Pension Backloading (Ippolito)

	Interest rate	Real pension wealth[a]		Percent of pension lost from quitting		Pension loss as a percent of wage	
Age		45	55	45	55	45	55
Service		10	20	10	20	10	20
	.025	$15,000	$30,000	39.3	22.1	59.0	66.3
	.050	15,000	30,000	63.3	39.3	94.5	117.9
	.100	15,000	30,000	86.4	63.3	129.6	189.9

SOURCE: Ippolito (1986, p. 143, table 8-3).
NOTE: Workers at age 45 have 10 years of service, and workers at age 55 have 20 years of service.
a. This is pension wealth as measured by projected liability.

A number of researchers concerned with the effects of pension backloading on benefit replacement rates examine the impact of workers moving between jobs and of holding more than one pension. In chapter 4 we show that for movers from pension-covered jobs, only a third have a new pension one year later, and just over a half have a new pension after five years. Thus pension losses from mobility are understated when it is assumed that all workers who had a pension with their initial job find a pension on their new job. Nevertheless, it is of interest to ask what these studies conclude about the likely pension losses due to mobility from jobs offering backloaded pensions, on the assumption of continuous pension coverage.[6]

Turner (1993, p. 53) cites results from a Hay/Huggins Study (1988), which took the basic turnover rates from the SCF by imputing turnover behavior from the tenure and pension coverage distributions. This study defines portability loss as the difference between 100 percent and the ratio, expressed as a percentage, of:

•the actual retirement benefit that the worker will receive from all employers, to

•the retirement benefit that the worker would have received if all years of covered employment had been credited under the last pension plan that covered the worker. (Hay/Huggins 1988, p. 4)

The study considers only the primary pension and assumes coverage by a comparable plan on subsequent jobs. The findings include pension portability losses of 14.8 percent for all workers and losses averaging 23.3 percent for workers with a loss. For a worker with 25 years of covered experience who has a pension of median generosity, this 23.3 percent loss translates to about 52 percent of wages.[7]

The Congressional Budget Office (1987, p. 35) has made analogous calculations of the effect of multiple job holding on replacement rates. As can be seen in table 3.2, at a 3 percent inflation rate, a pension paying 1.5 percent per year of service on the average of the last 5 years' salary results in a replacement rate of 46.5 percent for an individual who has 9 years of service in the first pension-covered job and then spent the next 31 years in a job offering the same pension. A second employee who spent 20 years in each job has a replacement rate of 41.1 percent, and an employee who spent 40 years in a single job has a replacement rate of 60 percent. If each dollar of annual benefits has an annuitized value of $12, then the annual loss of around 15 percent of final salary (the rough average of employees A and B) has a present value of about 1.8 times final salary (12 times 15 percent). This is an extreme example, though, because the 1.5 percent is higher than average and because the typical pension-covered worker will have considerably less than 40 years of covered experience at retirement.[8]

Of those who have calculated the pension loss from mobility, Allen, Clark, and McDermed employ an approach closest to the one we have taken in chapter 2. Recall that the pension backloading in table 2.4 represents a little over $17,000 in 1983 dollars. In comparison, Allen, Clark, and McDermed (1987) find an average loss for 35-44 year olds (our sample is 31-50 year olds) of $6,530 in 1974 dollars; that translates to $12,000 in 1983 dollars. All things considered, the findings of the two studies appear to agree reasonably well as to the general order of magnitude of the pension loss.[9]

Table 3.2 Effect of Length of Service on Defined Benefit Pensions (An Example)

Employee	Years of service, first job	Years of service, second job	Replacement rate on final five-year salary average (percent)
A	9	31	46.5
B	20	20	41.1
C	40	0	60.0

SOURCE: Congressional Budget Office (1987, p. 35, table 6).

Other studies have also calculated pension backloading. As discussed, the focus is more often on the effects of mobility on pension replacement rates when there are defined benefit plans or on the effects of mobility on the implicit promise made by the employer, than on the impact of pension backloading on mobility. Nevertheless, there have been a number of studies that have looked directly at the effects of pension backloading on mobility. Several other studies have assumed that the negative relationship between pension coverage and mobility must reflect backloading.

Hypotheses Explaining Why Firms Might Use Backloaded Pensions to Reduce Mobility

One possible explanation as to why firms might use pensions to reduce mobility is rooted in human capital theory. Some firms invest in workers by paying substantial hiring and training costs. Hence, these employers need to regulate turnover so as to guarantee a long enough payback period to warrant the investment in human capital. A negative pension-mobility link may be due to the efforts of the firm to reduce mobility incentives among those already employed.

A related hypothesis explaining adoption of defined benefit pensions is also motivated by the firm's desire to economize on hiring and training costs. Allen, Clark, and McDermed (1993) argue that firms use defined benefit pensions to influence self-selection by workers, with the aim of encouraging applications by those who are least likely to leave by virtue of their own preferences. If some workers are likely to be "stayers" while others are likely to be "movers," it will pay the firm to discriminate among these different types, sorting out those workers who, by preference, are movers. A bonus that is conditional on long-term attachment is worth less to a mover and will achieve the desired goal (Salop and Salop 1976). Thus, a desire to avoid the additional hiring and training costs associated with turnover may have motivated the firm to adopt backloaded pensions that impose a capital loss on those who leave the firm. This approach would discourage those on board from leaving and encourage those who are considering a job not to take it unless they intend to stay.

The pension capital loss may also be used to screen workers for other desirable characteristics, such as a willingness to work. A recent extension of the sorting theory by Ippolito (1993 and forthcoming b) posits that some workers have a higher time preference than do others and thus more heavily discount payments to be received in future periods. Low time-preference workers are also presumed to have some characteristic that is unobservable *ex ante* but valuable to the firm, such as higher productivity or lower turnover rates. If capital markets are imperfect and workers are on the margin of borrowing through the relevant period, low time-preference workers will value pensions even though they transform a portion of compensation into future income. Under these circumstances, a sharp difference in the imputed values of pensions will emerge between low and high time-preference workers. The difference in the valuation of a defined benefit and defined contribution plan will also be sharper in this situation because firms are less likely to cash out a defined benefit plan with any significant value than a defined contribution plan, for which a lump-sum settlement can often be obtained. This will also discourage high time-preference workers from seeking such jobs. Once a delayed payment mechanism is found to be appropriate, either for economizing on costs or for encouraging increased work effort, the pension, with its tax-deferred status, becomes an attractive vehicle for inducing the desired behavior.

Evidence on the Relationship of Pension Coverage to Turnover

There are two types of studies that have analyzed the relationship of pensions to turnover. One, which represents the majority of studies, examines the relationship of turnover or tenure to pension coverage on the job. A second type, discussed in the following section, attempts to estimate directly the effects of pension capital loss on turnover.

Table 3.3 presents results from probit analyses taken from one of the turnover equations estimated in Mitchell (1982, p. 295, table 3). Standard errors are reported in parentheses. The results, which are based on data from the 1973 and 1977 Quality of Employment Survey, show that there is a strong and significant negative relationship between pension coverage and turnover. The coefficient for males, which is the group analyzed in our mobility analysis, translates into a 20 percentage point difference in the mobility rates between individuals who are covered by a pension and those who are not.

Table 3.3 Relationship between Pension Coverage and Job Change for Males as Reported by Mitchell (1982)

	Males	Females
Coefficient on pension coverage variable in multivariate probit equation	-0.700[a] (0.155)	-0.519[a] (0.190)

SOURCE: Mitchell (1982, p. 295, table 3).
NOTE: Asymptotic standard errors are in parentheses.
a. Indicates a *t* statistic of 1.96 or better. The equations include race, education, union membership, experience, tenure, and wage as independent variables.

The differences in turnover for workers who are and are not covered by pensions has been known for many years.[10] It is well established that turnover is lower for workers covered by pension plans.[11] Turnover among workers with pension coverage is about half the rate for workers without pensions.[12] In 1983, length of service was 8.8 years for employees in the Current Population Survey whose employers provided a pension, while it was 4.1 years for workers in other jobs.[13] Allen, Clark, and McDermed (1991) survey a number of the studies in this area and emphasize that in the studies they review, "pension coverage has been the strongest correlate of mobility and length of service." They also present their own analysis, in which they find that turnover is negatively related to pension coverage, while reported job tenure is positively related to pension coverage, other variables constant.

Direct Analyses of the Relationship of Pension Backloading to Mobility

In addition to studies that focus on the relationship of pension coverage to turnover, there have been attempts to estimate directly the relationship of the pension capital loss to employee turnover. Allen, Clark, and McDermed (1993, p. 476) conclude that pension capital losses account for about 40 percent of the turnover difference between those with and without a pension.

They specify and estimate three equations using the 1975-82 Panel Study of Income Dynamics (PSID), with information on pension capital loss computed from a separate Employee Benefit Survey and matched to the PSID observations on the basis of occupation and industry. One equation, a selection equation, estimates the probability of being covered by a pension as a function of the probability of turnover from the pension-covered job. In another version of that equation, the probability of coverage is a function of a variable interacting the likelihood of the worker leaving a pension-covered job with a measure of pension capital loss. These specifications are meant to relate coverage to the expected cost of leaving the pension-covered job. The coverage equation also includes other controls. A second equation estimates the probability of leaving a pension-covered job in the seven-year period from 1975 to 1982 as a function of pension capital loss. The controls in this equation include a measure of hourly compensation that incorporates the prorated value of the accrued (stay) pension, i.e., a measure of pension value computed using the wage at retirement instead of the wage in the current period. The third equation estimates the probability of leaving a job that does not offer a pension as a function of a set of controls, including the wage. These equations are estimated jointly, and relationships among the unobservables from each equation are also considered.[14]

Allen, Clark, and McDermed's findings include the following:

1. A $1,000 increase in pension capital loss reduces turnover by 1.8 percentage points, so that the overall capital loss observed in the sam-

ple would account for 41 percent of the difference in turnover between those with and without pensions.

2. Workers with low odds of turnover self-select into pension-covered jobs, but they do so on the basis of observable rather than unobservable characteristics. Unobservables in the pension coverage equation are not correlated with either of the turnover equations.

3. The expected capital loss has little effect on the odds of being in a job with a pension. Neither the probability of turnover nor the interaction of the probability of turnover with capital loss is significant in the pension coverage equation.

It is important to emphasize that the correlations among the error terms are insignificant. Also, there is no significant effect of expected pension capital loss on pension coverage. This means that any selection into pension-covered jobs can be accommodated by estimating mobility equations without worrying about bias from selection into a pension-covered job, as long as the exogenous variables in the mobility equation include those observables that are associated with choosing pension-covered jobs. Consequently, Allen, Clark, and McDermed feel free to examine the effect of pension capital loss on quits and layoffs in a single equation mobility model.

Other Relevant Findings on the Pension-Mobility Relationship

In addition to the findings from basic pension-mobility studies, there are more detailed results germane to the pension-mobility relationship. Three are noted here. First, as emphasized by Allen, Clark, and McDermed (1993, p. 476), the strength of the estimated relationship between pensions and mobility declines with years of service. Second, as noted by Mitchell (1982) and as confirmed by Allen, Clark, and McDermed and others, pensions are more strongly related to layoffs than to quits, and thus are more strongly related to overall turnover than to quits. Moreover, when layoffs and quits are related to a measure of pension backloading by Allen, Clark, and McDermed, layoff probabilities fall by 1.3 percentage points for each $1,000 increase in capital loss, but the effect of a $1,000 capital loss is to reduce quits by less than one-half of 1 percentage point. Third, as recently found by Even and Macpherson (1992), the negative pension-mobility relationship holds up in large firms, but not in small firms, suggesting indirectly that the defined benefit plans more prevalent in larger firms are inhibiting mobility.

Questions About the Literature Findings

We now consider questions raised by the research that has been discussed. Specifically, we explain our doubt that backloaded defined benefit pensions account for a large part of the differences in mobility found between those who hold jobs offering pensions and those who hold jobs that do not.

Pension Backloading and Disincentives to Mobility

Despite the existence of a pension capital loss associated with backloading and special early retirement benefits, we doubt that pensions create sufficient incentives to account for the level and patterns of mobility observed. In our previous work (Gustman and Steinmeier 1987 and 1993b), and as emphasized by the calculations in chapter 2, we have noted that the disincentive to mobility created by defined benefit pensions is small enough to be easily overcome by a raise of a few percentage points on the new job.

Why Firms Might Use a Backloaded Pension to Reduce Mobility

The analysis in chapter 2 also shows that the pattern of penalties to mobility induced by defined benefit plans is not consistent with a hypothesis emphasizing the importance of reducing hiring and training costs. Larger penalties are created for those with greater experience. Yet those with fewer years on the job are precisely the workers the firm would like to discourage from moving, since early mobility on their part will create the least return to training and hiring costs. The small penalty to mobility for those who have just started on the job suggests that the firm probably does not count on the pension to reduce mobility in the years immediately after hiring and training costs are incurred.

It has also been argued that vesting is responsible for reduced turnover from pension-covered jobs. However, there are a number of unanswered questions about the relationship between vesting and mobility.

Before regulation from the Employee Retirement Income Security Act of 1974 (ERISA), the vesting period was quite long, often extending for a number of decades. This suggests that whatever its current purpose, vesting was not initially used by firms as a tool for offsetting training and hiring costs by reducing mobility of workers who were within the first decade of employment. Even now, the effect on mobility is likely to be small, although vesting rules do create a discontinuity in compensation accrual as the vesting period approaches. That is, given limitations on the vesting period under current law, which requires 5-year cliff vesting or graded vesting centered around the 5-year period, pension accruals are small enough at the time of vesting so that losses due to turnover during the first years of employment are likely to be slight (Kotlikoff and Wise 1985, 1987a). Direct calculations of the effects of a reduction in vesting from 10 to 5 years also suggest that recent changes in vesting rules, and related requirements for crediting work at young ages, are unlikely to affect incentives for turnover substantially (Gustman and Steinmeier 1989b).

The Relationship of Pension Coverage to Turnover

As noted, an important reason why researchers believe that pensions reduce mobility is that there is a strong correlation between pension coverage and measures of mobility or tenure. The fundamental question to be addressed is whether this correlation reflects causality, or whether important causal factors that generate the correlation have been omitted. Much of our work in this book addresses the question of what omitted variables might explain the correlation between pension coverage and mobility.

One candidate for the omitted variable has been suggested by the research of Allen, Clark, and McDermed. Their finding that pension backloading has a greater effect on layoffs than quits, along with Mitchell's earlier findings to the same effect, suggests that causality may run from the implicit contract, whatever its form and value, to mobility and pension design, rather than directly from pension backloading to mobility. That is, the implicit contract, and the productivity or rent-sharing arrangement underlying that contract, may be the omitted factor. Such an arrangement may lead to payment of a compensation premium on pension-covered jobs. That source of bias has been analyzed in our earlier work (Gustman and Steinmeier 1987, 1993b) and will be examined extensively in this book.

Direct Analyses of the Relationship of Pension Backloading to Mobility

The evidence in Allen, Clark, and McDermed (1993), that pension backloading is substantially responsible for the lower mobility from pension-covered jobs, is also characterized by a number of anomalies. The findings are not internally consistent and suggest the possibility of specification error in the model. In particular, the results imply that an additional dollar of pension capital loss would have over 20 times the effect on turnover as would an additional dollar of compensation. But why should an extra dollar realized in the form of pension backloading be so much more influential in reducing turnover than a dollar realized in the form of higher wages?

According to Allen, Clark, and McDermed, "The impact of a $1,000 increase in the capital loss is a 1.8 percentage point reduction in the odds of turnover" (1993, p. 476). They also find that "a one dollar increase in before-tax compensation is associated with a 1.8 percentage point decrease in the odds of turnover..." (p. 477). A flow of $1 per hour in wages translates into a present value of $20,000 to $30,000 in the 15-to-20 years until retirement. Accordingly, their findings suggest that a one-dollar pension capital loss has about 20 to 30 times the impact of one extra dollar received as wages. On the face of it, this result is implausible. It is likely that some omitted factor is correlated with their measure of pension backloading and with mobility. A complete specification of the model should produce results in which an extra dollar of compensation has a comparable effect on mobility, no matter what the source.[15]

Allen, Clark, and McDermed also find that all of the sorting into pension-covered jobs is based on observables, not on unobservables, and that "the expected magnitude of capital loss has little effect on the sorting of workers by pension coverage" (p. 476). This finding is puzzling since Allen, Clark, and McDermed believe that sorting would be a good candidate for the omitted variable that causes an overestimate of the correlation between pension backloading and mobility.[16] Moreover, simultaneous equations bias, proceeding from occupational choices and resulting characteristics associated with mobility, to pension backloading, might provide a plausible explanation for the differences in some mobility equation estimates. These differences would exist between the coefficients on pension backloading on the one hand and the measured effects of other differences in compensation on the other. However, their findings also rule out an effect of pension backloading on job choice.

In sum, there are a number of anomalies in the Allen, Clark, and McDermed studies of the relationship of pension backloading to mobility. These issues lead us to question a conclusion that backloading accounts for a substantial part of the reduction in mobility from pension-covered jobs.

Other Relevant Findings Suggested in the Literature on the Pension-Mobility Relationship

The finding in Allen, Clark, and McDermed (1991) that pension capital loss reduces mobility more for younger than for older workers accords with a model that emphasizes the importance of the pension as a device for reducing hiring costs. This finding does not, however, mesh with the time pattern of disincentives to mobility created by the standard plan formula, or by relevant results from pension surveys. Petersen (1992) and the evidence examined in chapter 2 suggest that the pattern of disincentives has a basic inverted U shape, rather than a declining pattern with age. The net effect is that the disincentives to mobility created by pensions are higher a decade or two after hiring than in the first few years after the date of hire. If the special early retirement benefits are considered, the pattern of disincentives may even be uniformly increasing with age. In this case, mobility should fall with tenure until the early retirement age, as found by Stock and Wise (1990).[17] Given the very weak penalty to mobility in early years, it is hard to rationalize an effect of pensions on mobility that is very large for workers with low tenure.[18]

The next questions for consideration are raised by findings that pension capital loss reduces turnover almost exclusively through its effect on (perhaps, correlation with) layoffs. Firms would have no reason to employ backloaded pensions to decrease mobility by reducing layoffs, since layoffs can be determined directly. It is possible to rationalize the relationship of pensions to layoffs as evidence for an implicit contract, in that there may be a linkage between pension capital loss and the firm's reluctance to break the contract and engage in layoffs. However, if this is true, the purpose of the implicit contract must be something other than reducing worker quits; otherwise, we would expect to see a decrease in the quit rate as well. For instance, firms might be using the implicit contract to reduce shirking or encourage more effort, and a diminished layoff rate may be necessary in order for workers to believe that they will get the expected future payoffs if they cooperate. This is no longer a story of pensions causing lower mobility; it is a story of pension and layoff policies being used together by the firms for a broader goal.

A related possibility is reverse causality, as firms shape pensions to meet turnover expectations for their covered workers. That is, selection of plan coverage or plan type may be a result, not only of the decisions of the workers, as in a mover-stayer model, but of the firm's efforts to provide a desirable vehicle for savings. It may be that at firms where turnover is likely to be higher, plans are arranged to accommodate the pattern of turnover. We know that this is a likely explanation for the prevalence of defined contribution plans in higher education, for example. Accordingly, while Allen, Clark, and McDermed find that expected turnover does not account for pension coverage, it still may be that those workers in jobs characterized by high rates of turnover are more likely to be covered by defined contribution plans, or defined benefit plans designed specifically to impose a lower penalty for turnover.[19]

A finding in favor of the hypothesis that pensions are used directly to reduce mobility is that the pension-mobility relationship persists in samples of large, but not in samples of small, firms. This is especially the case because pensions are more likely to be defined benefit in larger firms, and so they are more likely to be characterized by a significant pension capital loss with turnover.[20] Still, the fact that compensation and work conditions are so different between large and small firms (Brown and Medoff 1989) leaves open the possibility that there also is important omitted variable bias.

Further insight into the pension-mobility relationship might be gained by a more careful specification of the mobility equation, a specification that distinguishes among alternative explanations for mobility: changing information on the quality of a match, asymmetric information, changing demand patterns, reverse causation, or other reasons. The current models of the pension-mobility relationship have not yet specified equations that carefully model these separate factors.

Unresolved Issues

A number of issues in the literature on wage determination remain unresolved and, as a consequence, leave in doubt the relationships determining compensation and employment that underlie our findings. On the conceptual level, we know that wages and pensions are jointly determined, together with employment and worker costs and quality, where by quality we mean factors affecting various dimensions of productivity including skill and effort. Also to be considered are determinants of noncompensation costs, such as turnover. But we do not have a very good fix on how these various elements of firm labor demand are determined.

Some of the relevant relationships are suggested by standard considerations that arise from demand analysis in spot labor markets, but most of the considerations that would allow us to fully understand the determination of labor compensation, quantity, and quality in a model that incorporates pensions requires an analysis in the context of long-term job attachment between the worker and the firm. Institutions arise for influencing and adjudicating terms of employment, including but not limited to unions. With long-term job attachment, markets need not clear at each moment in time. Moreover, with long-term job attachment and property rights in the job, it becomes more reasonable to suppose that if there are any rents accruing to the firm, there is some possibility of workers capturing a portion of the rents.

With long-term attachment, there must be provision for changes in the economic environment. This has led to the idea of an implicit employment contract that would establish expected responses to the most common economic changes. Such arrangements may include, but are not restricted to, responses to various contingencies, ranging from the business cycle to the long-run success of the firm.

In addition, there may be special considerations that have shaped the role of the pension in the implicit employment contract. These unique influences include unions, a changing regulatory environment, the rise and spread of a true labor market innovation in the form of the pension, and economies of scale in the provisions of certain benefits.

Considerable uncertainty persists about the terms of these arrangements, however, either in a steady state environment or in one that is changing over time. As a result, there is uncertainty about what underlies the relationship between mobility, pensions, and the associated compensation changes that we are observing. We will find that workers who leave firms that offer pensions experience a compensation decline significantly larger than the wage decline experienced by those who leave jobs that do not offer pensions, but this finding remains subject to a number of interpretations.

One possibility is that jobs that offer pensions pay higher compensation than jobs that do not offer pensions. There is a long literature dating back to Slichter (1950) and his students that relates interindustry wage differentials to the presence of market power and rents received by firms. Certain jobs are "good jobs," providing individuals with relatively higher wages. This literature, which is summarized by Segal (1986), does not require that compensation differences be equalizing. Rather, the idea is that, in the face of imperfect competition, it is possible for wages not to be equalizing. Some of these differentials may constitute rents that exceed any compensation differentials intended to raise worker productivity.

The literature on dual labor markets (Cain 1976) has addressed in some detail the question of whether there are good and bad jobs. Tests of the dual labor market hypothesis analyze whether wage differentials reflect compensating wage differentials or unmeasured ability and whether only certain work rewards formal on-the-job training.

An additional step required, if it is to be established that wage premiums are more likely to accrue to pension-covered workers, is that high-wage jobs must have a higher propensity to offer pensions. The literature on pension coverage, and on coverage by defined benefit plans, does suggest that these plans are more likely to be offered to those in union jobs, in jobs in large firms, and in jobs in particular industries. (See Gustman and Mitchell 1992 and Gustman, Mitchell, and Steinmeier 1994 for surveys of the relevant evidence.)

A related literature, efficiency wage studies, argues that wage premiums are paid in certain industries and by certain firms as a method for increasing productivity. Thus, firms pay higher wages than the individual can obtain elsewhere as a way of maintaining worker discipline and work effort. In this case the worker does receive a wage premium over and above compensation on the next best job. At least some, and perhaps all, of the higher wage results from a compensating wage difference.

Some of the controversy about the payment of wage premiums has addressed the question of the optimal arrangement for structuring incentive pay. Lazear's work (1979, 1983) provides a basis for many discussions of incentive pay models where monitoring is costly, and it has the advantage of incorporating an explicit role for pensions. At issue is whether it is necessary to pay greater compensation in order to increase work effort, or whether it is sufficient to structure compensation so that at the time of hire workers post a bond and are repaid the value of the bond over the course of the employment arrangement. Akerlof and Katz (1989) argue, for example, that efficient bonding schemes are not possible and that the use of an up-front age-earnings profile as a mechanism for bonding is not fully efficient, so that in the presence of monitoring costs it will pay to offer efficiency wages.[21]

According to the traditional view on the supply side of the labor market, the payment of higher wages with tenure is explained by the presence of job-specific training (Becker 1964; Mincer 1974). Topel (1990) has attempted to estimate the size of wage loss when turnover causes forfeiture of specific human capital. Other forms of investment that might result in a wage loss with turnover include the effort in obtaining an optimal job match (Jovanovic 1979a and b). Although it is clear that specific investment should raise the post-training wage of those who have engaged in such activity, it is not clear why specific training should raise the value of lifetime earnings net of costs. If the costs and benefits from such training are shared, a worker of a given quality should receive the same lifetime compensation as would be received in other employment that did not involve specific training.

In order to better understand the wage determination process, and the reasons for wage differences with turnover, we need to improve our comprehension not only of the determination of compensation differences among jobs, but of the relationship between compensation and tenure on a given job. The question of what underlies the wage tenure, or compensation tenure, profile is fundamental to understanding how compensation is determined over the period of job attachment. This is an unsettled issue. Some argue that apparent seniority premiums that have been attributed to specific training are really the result of selection bias. Relevant references to this debate include Abraham and Farber (1985, 1987), Altonji and Shakotko (1987), and Topel (1986, 1990).

An obvious question is whether those who appear to be receiving a wage premium are really being paid for some unobservable dimension of higher quality. There have been a number of efforts to determine whether those who are receiving higher wages are more desirable to the firm. One basic idea is to look at job movers and to see whether those who appear to be receiving a wage premium actually receive a higher wage in alternative employment. Refinements of this idea have been developed in studies analyzing the differences in wage changes for those who leave their old jobs for various reasons (Gibbons and Katz 1989, 1991). None of the relevant studies has been able to explain the wage differentials observed for employees in particular industries, or at larger firms, by resorting to unmeasured individual characteristics. That is, workers from particular industries and large firms typically categorized as high-wage employers do experience larger wage declines than do workers from low-wage industries or smaller firms, even controlling for the reason for job change.

Ippolito (forthcoming b) has used the idea of worker heterogeneity to explain pension backloading. He theorizes that the firm uses the backloaded pension to sort out workers with different degrees of time preference and that time preference of workers is correlated with other worker characteristics, which are then related to turnover. The direct evidence we have discussed finds no relationship between turnover and unmeasured worker characteristics, and there is as yet no empirical support for Ippolito's conjectures on the relationship of pensions to such characteristics.

Studies of compensating wage differentials are directly germane to the question of how pensions relate to compensation. That literature has not been especially successful in isolating compensating wage differentials for job conditions (Brown 1980). There also have been special efforts to isolate compensating wage differentials for pensions. Most studies find a positive relationship between pension coverage and wages (Gordon and Blinder 1980), and between pension values and wages (Gustman and Steinmeier 1989a). Recent work has attempted to apply hedonic techniques to isolate the pension-wage tradeoff. It suggests that if productivity is held constant, a negative tradeoff between pensions and wages might be generated. However, identification of exogenous instruments has been a real problem. Thus, the leading work in this area, Montgomery, Shaw, and Benedict (1992), for example, uses pension characteristics as instruments in the estimation. The pension plan features are jointly determined with the wage and pension level, however, and are thus endogenously determined.

It might be argued that older job changers face special disadvantages. Barnow and Ehrenberg (1979) show that one consequence of backloaded pensions is that a firm's pension costs are greater when it hires older workers. It has also been argued that firms are unwilling to invest in the specific training for older workers that they are willing to provide for younger workers. Older workers are attached to the firm for fewer years, and thus the firm has less time to recapture its investment (Hutchens 1986). Because workers who share in the returns to specific investment are also expected to invest in specific training, it is not clear why the net present value of older job losers' compensation streams should necessarily be reduced as a result of the firm's unwillingness to invest in their training. Indeed, if the older job mover were being trained upon initial hire, shared investment activities would depress rather than increase the observed wage. A possible explanation is that workers are valuable to the firm only if the firm can also invest in their specific training. Alternatively, there must be something else about the relationship between the net wage paid to the worker and the type of job that accounts for the decline in wages observed with turnover of older workers.

There are interactions among these various models. The specific training literature focuses our attention on job training at the beginning of the period of employment (Oi 1983). However, as we will continue to argue, it is unlikely that pensions create incentives that would allow the firm to economize on hiring and training costs at the time of initial hire. Others, such as Ippolito in the studies noted previously, argue that training takes place throughout the period of job attachment. Thus, pensions that discourage turnover among more mature workers are, nevertheless, economizing on training costs. While new CPS data have become available on training activity by workers and there is useful data from the National Longitudinal Surveys of Labor Market Experience (NLS), we have no consensus on the distribution of specific training over the course of job attachment.[22]

In sum, the research has not yet clearly explained compensation differences in the labor market, particularly those differences between jobs offering pensions and jobs without pensions. A better understanding of this phenomenon is needed in order to determine what mechanism accounts for the decline in compensation with turnover from pension-covered jobs. The outstanding questions are fundamental to labor economics, and we are not able to resolve them here.

In the remainder of the book we will present evidence that there is an important omitted factor from studies of the relationship of pension incentives to mobility. Further, the evidence suggests the omitted factor is a compensation premium paid on pension-covered jobs. This chapter has laid a foundation for that finding. It has suggested a number of problems with the current literature on the pension-mobility relationship, and also indicates that payment of a wage premium on pension-covered jobs is consistent with other findings in labor economics.

NOTES

1. The analysis in this chapter draws heavily on our own previous published work, Gustman and Steinmeier 1993b, as well as on studies we have completed with Olivia Mitchell (Gustman and Mitchell 1992 and Gustman, Mitchell, and Steinmeier 1993 and 1994).

2. There are other benefit formulas, such those typical in the union sector, in which a flat dollar payment is given for each year of service. These dollar amounts are increased from one contract to the next, so that the plans mimic pensions in which benefits are based on final average salary or lifetime earnings. Workers who leave such plans early also suffer the analog of a pension capital loss.

3. A central question is whether the firm's pension liability should be the legal liability, in which case the benefit accrued to date is the pension amount owed on the assumption that today is the worker's last day of employment. Alternatively, the pension liability could be calculated assuming the worker continues employment at the firm; the pension liability would be evaluated using the wage projected at the time of retirement. Under current actuarial practice, the projected liability is used. Bulow (1982) argues for use of the legal liability concept, while Ippolito (1986) argues for use of the projected liability and the existence of an implicit employment contract. For calculations of the differences in the liabilities, which are a direct reflection of pension backloading, see Gustman and Steinmeier (1989a).

4. That is, the assumption that pensions are paid as a lump sum at the beginning of the retirement period, and that the equivalent of the lump-sum payment determined by a given wage history does not vary with the inflation rate, is tantamount to assuming that benefits are fully indexed after retirement. The evidence suggests that between one-third and one-half of benefits in retire-

ment have been indexed (Allen, Clark, and Sumner 1986; Gustman and Steinmeier 1993a). The data in chapter 2 are based on the assumption of partial indexing of benefits after retirement.

5. In the example, the individual would receive $45,000 (15 percent of $10,000 times 30) upon retirement at 65. The present value of wages would be $300,000 (30 times $10,000). Thus, the pension amounts to 15 percent of the value of his wages over the period, which would place this individual at almost the 75th percentile among the actual SCF pension-covered workers in table 2.3.

6. As we also note, some of those who did not have a pension on their initial job do find a pension on their new jobs. For that reason, compensation gain is missed when it is assumed that pension status remains unchanged with mobility.

7. According to table 2.3, median pension wealth for individuals in the 55-65 age range is about 9 percent of wage wealth. This means that an individual with 25 years of covered employment would have pension wealth equal to about 2.25 times annual earnings (.09 times 25). Thus a loss of 23.3 percent of pension wealth would result in a loss of about 52 percent of annual earnings (.233 times 2.25).

8. Given these figures, the total value of the pension would be equal to 7.2 years of earnings (12 times the 60 percent replacement rate if the worker does not leave the firm), or about 18 percent of the earnings over the working life (7.2 of 40 years). This compares to a median value of 9 percent for 55-65 year-old workers in table 2.3. For a worker who has been on the job for 15 years and has another 15 years to go until retirement, the replacement rate would be 45 percent if the worker continues in the same job until retirement and 36.75 percent if he or she changes jobs. This produces a benefit loss of only 8 percent versus the considerably larger losses shown in table 3.2.

9. The estimates of backloading by Allen, Clark, and McDermed (1987) involve some understatement. Specifically, their procedure does not catch the spikes in the accrual profile, which we found in table 2.3 to be sizable. It also seems likely that pension generosity increased to some degree between 1974 and 1983.

10. See Ross (1958) and the U.S. Department of Labor (1964).

11. See also Ippolito (1987), among others.

12. For example, in the sample from the Survey of Income and Program Participation (SIPP) that we examine, one-year mobility rates were about 20 percent for those without pensions and 6 percent for those with pensions. Five-year mobility rates were 57.8 and 32.4 percent, respectively, in the PSID.

13. Allen, Clark, and McDermed (1993).

14. To be more specific, the three equations estimated by Allen, Clark, and McDermed are as follows, in the original notation:

$$P_i^* = \beta_{11}' X_{1i} + B_{12} \tilde{T}_{Pi} \cdot CL_i + \varepsilon_{1i}$$
$$T_{pi}^* = \beta_{21}' X_{2i} + B_{22} CL_i + \varepsilon_{2i}$$
$$T_{Ni}^* = \beta_{31}' X_{3i} + \varepsilon_{3i}$$

where P_i^* is a latent variable indicating the odds that a particular worker will be covered by a pension; T_{pi}^* and T_{Ni}^* are latent variables indicating the odds of leaving a job with a pension (P) and without a pension (N); X_{1i}, X_{2i} and X_{3i} are vectors of control variables; and $\tilde{T}_{Pi} = \text{Prob}\,(T_{Pi}^* > 0)$ (Allen, Clark, and McDermed, 1993, p. 467). The error terms are normally distributed, with non-zero covariances between ε_{1i} and ε_{2i} and between ε_{1i} and ε_{3i}, but, with zero covariance between ε_{2i} and ε_{3i}.

15. It would be appropriate to adjust for differences in risk among sources of compensation, but, due to unexpected turnover, potential income from backloading of pensions appears to be a

highly risky element of compensation. Accordingly, failure to adjust for risk should lead to an overstatement rather than an understatement of the importance of pension backloading as an influence on mobility.

16. If this finding is accepted, a direct implication is that a single-equation mobility model may be applied to an analysis of mobility from pension and nonpension jobs without causing bias. This conclusion is consistent with the approach of Allen, Clark, and McDermed in examining the relationship of pensions to quits and layoffs. The only requirement is that observable variables associated with selection into pension-covered jobs be held constant.

17. In the Allen, Clark, and McDermed (1991) study, covering the 1975 to 1982 period, the mean pension capital loss from turnover is $821 for those under age 25, $2,926 for those between 25 and 34, $6,526 for those between 35 and 44, and $8,503 for those 45 to 54.

18. Allen, Clark, and McDermed (1991) suggest that the negative effect of pensions on mobility of younger workers is due to selection, in which stayers are more likely to accept pension-covered jobs because they defer earnings, and that the effect of this self-selection is more likely to show up at younger ages. This implies that young workers who are stayers must impute great value to the expected pension, despite the very small cost of leaving the firm in the first few years of employment. However, their own results show that expected pension capital loss has no effect on selection into pension-covered jobs This suggests that if selection is important, it works when those with the observable characteristics of stayers choose pension-covered jobs, whatever the incentives from backloading.

19. Consistent with this view, Dorsey (1987) finds that, among manufacturing industries, the probability of coverage by a defined contribution plan is positively related to the layoff rate in the industry. This conclusion is also consistent with a view that firms reduce layoffs where there is an obligation under the implicit contract.

20. Estimates of the relationship between coverage and turnover, even when standardizing for plan type, provide only limited information about causality. Thus, in analyzing variation in the pension-mobility relationship with firm size, Even and Macpherson (1992) conclude that "... once the type of pension plan is controlled for, the effect of pensions on tenure varies less systematically with employer size, though there is weak evidence that DB plans have a greater effect at larger employers." More precise findings require use of direct information on plan incentives.

21. Related references on the efficiency wage controversy include Krueger and Summers (1987, 1988), Dickens and Katz (1987), and Katz and Summers (1989).

22. For a recent survey of what is known from the NLS data about training over the life cycle, see Light (1994).

4
Descriptive Data
and Multivariate Analyses

This chapter presents some basic descriptive findings pertaining to the relationship between pensions, job mobility, and wages. These results take the form of cross tabs and simple multivariate analyses and suggest the following conclusions:

- Workers on pension-covered jobs exhibit lower turnover than those on nonpension jobs.

- Workers with pensions have higher wages and thus even higher compensation than those without pensions.

- Wage losses are greater for movers from pension-covered than from nonpension jobs.

- Movers from jobs with pensions are more likely than movers from jobs without pensions to locate a pension on their new jobs. Nevertheless, when pensions are considered, they increase the relative compensation loss for movers from pension jobs and raise the compensation gain for movers from nonpension jobs.

- Defined contribution plans, which are not backloaded, have the same negative association with mobility as do defined benefit plans, which are backloaded.

The Data

The data used in this chapter are from three surveys: (1) the 1983 Survey of Consumer Finances (SCF), which has retrospective data to analyze mobility between 1978 and 1983; (2) the Survey of Income and Program Participation (SIPP), which has panel data covering mobility over the period from 1984 to 1985; and (3) the Panel Study of Income Dynamics (PSID), which has panel data on mobility from 1984 and 1989.[1]

The data available in the three surveys are not comparable along a number of dimensions. The SCF is the only one of the surveys to have a matched employer-provided description of the pension plan attached to the survey responses of covered workers. These were obtained by asking the survey respondent the name of the employer and by then writing to the employer or searching U.S. Department of Labor files for the plan description. For the SIPP and PSID data, plan descriptions are matched on the basis of job characteristics from the sample of SCF plan descriptions. All three surveys indicate whether the individual is covered by a pension; however, the SCF and SIPP are the only surveys to contain usable self-reported information on plan type, along with other pension characteristics as described by the covered individual. The PSID collected information on plan type and other details of the pension from covered individuals, but it did so only for those age 45 and over. As a result, self-reported pension information is missing for most of the age range of interest for our mobility analysis. On the other hand, information on the reason for separation is available for the full sample in the PSID, but it is only selectively available in the other surveys, if at all.[2]

The SCF observations are based on interviews in 1983, which obtained retrospective information on job history. The base period was 1978. The survey asked about the wage and other characteristics of the 1978 job only if that job involved a pension or if it was the individual's longest prior job. Given this format, information on the wage and characteristics of the 1978 job is unavailable for some individuals. Accordingly, some of the simple base-period descriptive relationships can be calculated only for the true panels (SIPP and PSID) and not for the SCF data. Although censoring limits the availability of descriptive statistics for the retrospective SCF data, the structural analysis corrects for this problem econometrically and thus allows consistent estimation of compensation and its components on the 1978 job.

For the SIPP sample, the first interview was in 1983. The 1983 panel was interviewed every four months for two and a half years. The fourth and seventh interviews, conducted one year apart in 1984 and 1985, contain topical modules with questions pertaining to the individual's pension. Those interviews are the ones used here. For all individuals in the survey, the fourth interview covers a period in 1984, and the seventh covers a period in 1985. Some supplementary information from the third, fifth, and sixth interviews is also utilized.

The PSID sample works with information that was collected primarily in 1984 and 1989, although again some use is made of information collected in the intervening years (such as the reason for leaving the 1984 job, if that occurred). The 1984 and 1989 interviews provide information on current pension coverage, which is not available for any of the intermediate years.

Males were selected in each sample who were 31-50 years old at the beginning of the sample period.[3] To be eligible for selection, individuals had to be employed for at least 30 hours per week in private sector, nonagricultural firms at the beginning of the period. The study examines the mobility of prime-aged workers.[4] It does not consider the mobility of younger workers who are in the early stages of job search, nor does it consider the age range in which job change may be related to retirement or contemplation of retirement.

Four potential sources of differences among the surveys may be noted. First, the surveys cover different years. There is evidence that mobility at the end of the 1980s was different from mobility in earlier years.[5] The data are not sufficient for us to separate the effects of the survey year on the outcomes of interest, but it may be that differences in the results between the PSID and the two other surveys are partly a reflection of differences in the year of the survey.[6] Second, the period over which mobility is measured is shorter in the SIPP sample. Less mobility is observable over a shorter period, and those workers with multiple separations receive more weight in a shorter than in a longer period.[7] Third, SCF job change information is based on retrospective data, while for the PSID and SIPP, true panel data are available.[8] Fourth, the employer-provided pension information, which is not discussed in this chapter but is used in the structural analysis of chapters 6 and 7, is obtained from the individual's employer in the SCF but must be matched on the basis of other reported characteristics in the PSID or SIPP.[9]

The Findings

Turnover

Table 4.1 presents descriptive data on mobility, wages, and pensions using information from the three surveys.[10] Relative mobility from non-pension jobs is considerably higher than it is from pension jobs in each of the surveys, but the differences in mobility rates are much larger in the retrospective SCF data than they are in the panel data sets. The descriptive statistics from the SCF presented in table 4.1 suggest that males 31-50 years old without pensions are over six times as likely to move as those with pensions (59.1 percent versus 8.6 percent). SIPP data indicate that individuals initially without pensions are over three times more likely (19.5 percent versus 6.1 percent) to move from the 1984 job than are individuals with pensions. The PSID data exhibit turnover rates of 57.8 percent for those in a nonpension job and 32.4 percent for those in a pension job over a five-year period, indicating a slightly less than two-to-one ratio of mobility rates in accordance with pension status.

The relative differences among surveys in mobility rates of those without pensions are not large, considering that the SCF and PSID both cover five-year periods, while the SIPP covers only a one-year period. They are particularly close between the PSID and SCF samples, which calculate mobility over a five-year period. Differences in the relative mobility rates among pension-covered workers are more substantial. It is possible that differences in the time periods covered may account for some of the discrepancies. An alternative explanation is that the SCF asked specifically about any previous job with a pension. If the job history did not include 1978, the individual was presumed to have been working in a nonpension job at that time. If individuals who left pension jobs held in 1978 did not report those jobs (this question was at the tail end of a job history section), the mobility rate from pension jobs would be biased downward.

Table 4.2 presents estimates of the relationship between pension coverage and mobility from multivariate equations relating turnover to pension coverage.[11] These equations allow us to standardize for the effects of observable differences among individuals that may be corre-

Table 4.1 Mobility, Wages, and Pension Data for Males 31 to 50 Years Old, from the SCF, SIPP, and PSID

Survey	No pension in initial job		Pension in initial job	
	Stayers	**Movers**	**Stayers**	**Movers**
1978-83 SCF[a]				
Number of movers and stayers	106	153	338	32
Percent movers	59.1%		8.6%	
Mean wage in 1978 (initial job)	$8.19	$8.93	$11.91	$12.63
Mean wage in 1983	d	$9.11	d	$10.30
Percent with pension in 1983	d	38.6%	d	43.8%
1984-85 SIPP[b]				
Number of movers and stayers	803	195	1,646	107
Percent movers	19.5%		6.1%	
Mean wage in 1984 (initial job)	$8.71	$7.72	$11.88	$11.22
Mean wage in 1985	$8.86	$8.23	$11.89	$10.52
Percent with pension in 1985	d	13.8%	d	35.8%
Primary 1984 plan was defined benefit	d	d	64.3%	63.6%
1984-89 PSIDc				
Number of movers and stayers	79	118	263	126
Percent movers	57.8%		32.4%	
Mean wage in 1984 (initial job)	$9.19	$9.35	$12.92	$11.85
Mean wage in 1989	$9.95	$9.12	$13.09	$10.59
Percent with pension in 1989	d	37.0%	d	53.2%

a. Data from the SCF are based on the authors' computations. Wages are indexed to 1983 by the Index of Hourly Earnings (1988 *Economic Report of the President*, table B-44).
b. SIPP figures are from Gustman and Steinmeier (1993b, table 1), and from our own computations. Wages are indexed to 1984 by the Index of Hourly Earnings (1988 *Economic Report of the President*, table B-44).
c. Data from the PSID are based on the authors' computations. Wages are indexed to 1984 by the Wage and Salary Employment Cost Index (1991 *Economic Report of the President*, table B-45).
d. Not applicable.

lated with pension coverage and account for some of the observed differences in mobility between workers with and without pensions. As can be seen, the relationship between pension coverage and mobility is significant in all three probits. According the SCF retrospective data, those workers with pensions are 57 percent less likely to show turnover than those without pensions. The SIPP data indicate that the difference in turnover is 9 percent at the means for the one-year period covered. In the PSID panel, the turnover rate is 21 percent lower for pension-covered workers. Thus, the negative relationship of pension coverage to turnover is much stronger in the retrospective SCF data.

Table 4.2 Effects of Pension Coverage in Reduced Form Mobility Equations

1978-83 SCF	1984-85 SIPP	1984-89 PSID
-0.57	-0.09	-0.21
(10.90)	(6.50)	(4.24)

NOTES: Dependent variable is 1 if the individual separates and is 0 otherwise. Entries are probit marginal effects of the probability of separation for males age 31-50 in the initial year. Absolute values of asymptotic t statistics are given in parentheses. Other independent variables in the equations are indicated in appendix table 4.3.

Wages and Compensation

Line 3 of each panel of table 4.1 indicates the wages for movers and stayers, classified by pension coverage on their initial jobs. The results based on SCF data suggest that, in their initial jobs, stayers with pensions earned about 45 percent more than did stayers without pensions. In the SIPP data, stayers with pensions earned 36 percent more than stayers without pensions in their initial jobs, while in the PSID data they earned 41 percent more. Movers from pension-covered employment earned 45 percent more in their initial jobs than movers from nonpension jobs in the SIPP, and 27 percent more in the PSID. In the SCF data, the differential was 41 percent. Were the pensions evaluated, as they are in later chapters, and the value of the pension added to the wage differential, the resulting compensation margin in favor of pension-covered workers would be even wider.

There is an obvious question about the wage differentials between those workers with and without pensions. Are these wage differentials due to individual characteristics that enhance productivity, or do workers in pension-covered jobs receive wage premiums that may affect mobility? That is, to what extent, if any, will the higher wages of pension-covered workers on their initial jobs carry over into their opportunities on alternative jobs?

Suppose that the entire compensation differential between workers with and without pensions were due to individual characteristics, such as unmeasured ability. In this circumstance, the compensation on any alternative job would be identical to the compensation on the current job. We should not find, as we do, that pension workers face worse alternatives (relative to their current jobs) than nonpension workers.

Consider the other extreme. Suppose that compensation on the current job were entirely a reflection of the job rather than the person. Equivalent workers would be paid more on some jobs (e.g., pension jobs) than on others (e.g., nonpension jobs), either as a result of rent sharing or because of some productivity-enhancing scheme that calls for above-market wages.[12] In this case, the compensation difference between the pension and nonpension workers would indicate the difference in mobility disincentives among otherwise identical workers. Indeed, in a mobility equation the compensation level on the current job would standardize appropriately for any difference in mobility incentives facing workers on different jobs.[13]

It is possible, of course, that the compensation of workers on their current jobs is due to a mix of both explanations, unmeasured individual characteristics and differences in the compensation offered to otherwise identical workers. To isolate the incentive for mobility between the current job and other jobs, one would need an explicit estimate of all the factors shaping differences between the current and the opportunity wage. Information on the current wage alone would not be sufficient to control for the compensation differential associated with moving.

Tables 4.3 and 4.4 present estimates of standard wage equations for the initial period in the two panel data sets.[14] The first two equations are for workers in nonpension and pension jobs, respectively, and the final equation is for the whole sample. The coefficients for the pension variables in the two data sets indicate that workers in pension jobs receive over 16 percent more in wages in the SIPP, holding observable charac-

Table 4.3 Estimates of Wage Equations from the SIPP Data

Variable	Estimate (*t* statistic)		
	Jobs without pensions	Jobs with pensions	All jobs
Job characteristics			
Pension	a	a	0.164 (8.00)
Union	0.173 (3.29)	0.001 (0.05)	0.060 (2.85)
Firm size > 100	0.023 (0.68)	0.060 (2.39)	0.044 (2.19)
Industry			
Mining	0.039 (0.24)	0.078 (1.03)	0.066 (0.92)
Construction	0.048 (0.76)	0.307 (7.16)	0.175 (5.00)
Nondurable manufacturing	0.009 (0.15)	-0.068 (2.44)	-0.042 (1.56)
Transportation, communication & public utilities	0.000 (0.00)	0.037 (1.22)	0.031 (1.06)
Wholesale trade	-0.038 (0.57)	-0.053 (1.39)	-0.035 (1.04)
Retail trade	-0.238 (4.31)	-0.206 (5.75)	-0.217 (7.23)
Finance, insurance & real estate	0.062 (0.79)	0.055 (1.26)	0.071 (1.81)
Services	-0.165 (3.13)	-0.137 (3.95)	-0.113 (4.98)
Personal characteristics			
Experience (x 0.01)	0.910 (0.85)	0.103 (0.14)	0.417 (0.70)
Experience squared (x 0.001)	-0.179 (1.41)	-0.044 (0.54)	-0.087 (1.26)
Tenure (x 0.01)	3.744 (2.43)	0.147 (0.18)	1.531 (2.20)

Tenure squared (x 0.001)	-0.649	(2.09)	-0.368	(2.55)	-0.425	(3.25)
Education (x 0.1)	-0.434	(1.36)	-0.261	(1.33)	-0.204	(1.22)
Education squared (x 0.01)	0.494	(4.50)	0.245	(3.60)	0.307	(5.25)
Experience * education (x 0.001)	0.503	(0.70)	0.433	(0.94)	0.441	(1.13)
Tenure * education (x 0.001)	-1.278	(1.23)	1.318	(2.62)	0.273	(0.62)
Married	0.090	(2.26)	0.066	(2.45)	0.074	(3.29)
Poor health	0.024	(0.34)	-0.194	(4.48)	-0.115	(3.07)
Black	-0.168	(2.60)	-0.187	(4.86)	-0.182	(5.40)
Region						
North Central	-0.041	(0.86)	-0.040	(1.62)	-0.038	(1.68)
South	-0.044	(0.99)	-0.026	(1.01)	-0.040	(1.76)
West	0.057	(1.13)	0.036	(1.25)	0.047	(1.85)
Constant	1.533	(5.74)	2.045	(11.69)	1.639	(11.30)
R^2	0.262		0.262		0.315	
Number of observations	870		1,677		2,547	

NOTES: Absolute t statistics are in parentheses. Dependent variable is natural log of the hourly wage. Durable manufacturing is the omitted industry.
a. Not applicable.

Table 4.4 Estimates of Wage Equations from the PSID Data

Variable	Jobs without pensions		Jobs with pensions		All jobs	
	Estimate	(*t* statistic)	Estimate	(*t* statistic)	Estimate	(*t* statistic)
Job characteristics						
Pension	a		a		0.143	(4.24)
Union	0.362	(2.98)	-0.001	(0.04)	0.050	(1.40)
Industry						
Mining	0.096	(0.48)	0.146	(1.07)	0.105	(0.94)
Construction	0.259	(2.73)	0.138	(1.97)	0.179	(3.30)
Transportation, communication & public utilities	0.065	(0.65)	0.105	(2.51)	0.111	(2.86)
Trade	-0.101	(1.23)	-0.171	(3.32)	-0.153	(3.55)
Finance, insurance & real estate	0.239	(1.49)	-0.096	(1.13)	-0.008	(0.11)
Services	-0.069	(0.78)	-0.196	(3.63)	-0.137	(3.00)
Personal characteristics						
Experience (x 0.01)	3.000	(0.86)	0.943	(0.52)	1.166	(0.72)
Experience squared (x 0.001)	-0.699	(1.55)	-0.167	(0.68)	-0.203	(0.94)
Tenure (x 0.01)	-1.861	(0.67)	1.194	(0.83)	1.525	(1.30)
Tenure squared (x 0.001)	0.046	(0.10)	-0.129	(0.66)	-0.184	(1.04)
Education (x 0.1)	-1.457	(1.17)	-0.901	(1.49)	-0.681	(1.27)
Education squared (x 0.01)	0.966	(2.36)	0.617	(3.16)	0.596	(3.45)

Experience * education (x 0.001)	0.194	(0.11)	0.479	(0.48)	0.353	(0.42)
Tenure * education (x 0.001)	1.993	(1.04)	-0.094	(0.10)	-0.188	(0.24)
Married	-0.015	(0.21)	0.013	(0.24)	0.020	(0.47)
Poor health	0.160	(1.35)	-0.193	(3.04)	-0.120	(2.13)
Black	-0.271	(1.86)	-0.215	(3.13)	-0.207	(3.32)
Region						
Northeast	0.093	(1.08)	0.058	(1.39)	0.064	(1.68)
South	-0.118	(1.55)	-0.063	(1.57)	-0.091	(2.55)
West	-0.099	(1.07)	0.059	(1.25)	0.022	(0.51)
SMSA	0.165	(2.73)	0.086	(2.59)	0.096	(3.28)
Constant	2.042	(2.00)	2.260	(4.50)	1.819	(4.04)
R^2	0.488		0.392		0.442	
Number of observations	193		477		670	

NOTES: Absolute *t* statistics are in parentheses. Dependent variable is natural log of the hourly wage. Manufacturing is the omitted industry.
a. Not applicable.

teristics of the individual and the job constant, while for the PSID the comparable figure is over 14 percent. These figures are fairly typical for wage regressions of this type. It is, of course, an open question as to whether the higher wage for pension-covered jobs is economic rent or is compensation for unobservable worker characteristics not correlated with the observable variables.

These wage equations, along with analogous equations estimated for 1983 for the SCF, provide the experience and tenure coefficients needed to project wages. This projection, in turn, provides the basis for the compensation amounts used later in the analysis (and previously in the descriptive tables 2.3 and 2.4). For the SIPP, standard statistical tests indicate that the wage equations for workers with and without pensions are significantly different from one another, so separate equations are used in the later analysis. For the PSID, the test for differences between the equations for those with and without pensions is on the margin at 5 percent significance, and further tests indicate that the interaction terms between experience, tenure, and education are not jointly significant.[15] In view of the relatively small number of observations in the equation for workers without pensions, the combined equation is (without the interaction terms) employed to obtain the compensation amounts.

Wage Changes for Movers

We now turn to the data on wage changes for movers. The fourth line in each panel in table 4.1 indicates the wages at the end of the period, and a comparison of these figures with the third line yields the wage changes over the period.[16] Figure 4.1 depicts the changes in the wages for movers from pension and nonpension jobs in all three surveys, as calculated from the data in table 4.1.

Movers from pension jobs in all three surveys experience losses, while there are gains to movers from nonpension jobs in the SCF and the SIPP, and much smaller losses to movers from nonpension than pension jobs in the PSID. (Stayers in the two panel data sets, both those initially with and without pensions, experience small wage gains.) Relative to the wage in their old jobs, movers from nonpension jobs fare 8.1 percentage points better than movers from pension jobs in the PSID. In the SIPP, they fare 12.8 percentage points better, while in the SCF, they fare a whopping 20.4 percentage points better. These descriptive data certainly suggest that those who leave pension jobs fare relatively worse than do those who leave nonpension jobs.

Figure 4.1   Wage Changes for Movers

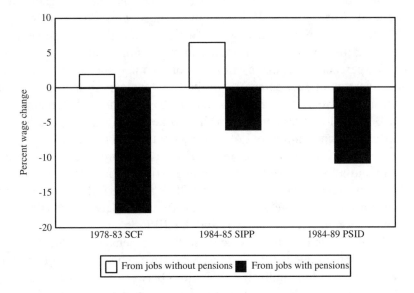

Pensions and Compensation Changes for Movers

An additional outcome of interest is the relative success of movers from pension-covered employment and of movers from jobs that did not initially offer a pension in securing new jobs that provide a pension. From the fifth row of each of the panels in table 4.1, it can be seen that 36 to 53 percent of those who left a pension job located new employment that included a pension. This means that about half of those who left a pension job lost pension coverage on their new job. On the other hand, 14 to 39 percent of those who left a nonpension job gained a pension coverage. The net effect of considering pensions in compensation change is to increase the relative compensation loss for movers from pension jobs and the compensation gains for those who left nonpension jobs.

Calculations from the 1983 SCF suggests that pensions are worth an average of 12.9 percent of compensation until retirement. In the SIPP, 13.8 percent of movers from jobs without pensions found pensions on their new jobs. The effect is to increase the size of the average compensation gain by 1.8 percentage points (13.8 percent of 12.9 percent). As compared to the wage gain of 6.6 percent, the compensation gain is 8.4 percent. Analogously, 35.8 percent of those who left a pension job locate a pension on their new job, which means that 62.4 percent do not. For these workers, consideration of pensions widens a wage loss of 6.2 percent to a compensation loss of 15.5 percent (6.2 percent plus 64.2 percent of 12.9 percent). For the PSID, movers from jobs without pensions have a compensation gain of 2.3 percent (-2.5 percent plus 37.0 percent of 12.9 percent), while workers who leave a pension job suffer a compensation loss of 16.6 percent (-10.6 percent minus 46.8 percent of 12.9 percent). For the SCF, the two figures are a 7.0 percent gain and a 29.6 percent loss for movers from jobs with and without pensions, respectively. For both the SIPP and the PSID, the effect of pensions approximately doubles the differential between pension and nonpension movers in the PSID and the SIPP.

Multivariate results for success in finding pensions in the new job tell much the same story. For those who have changed jobs, the partial relationships from multivariate equations between pension coverage on the initial job and on the new job are reported in table 4.5.[17] These

Table 4.5 Effects of Pension Coverage in Initial Job on Pension Coverage in New Job

	Estimate (*t* statistic)	
	1984-85 SIPP	1984-89 PSID
Pension coverage	0.117 (1.79)	0.121 (1.61)

NOTES: Table entries are marginal effects from probit estimates. Absolute values of asymptotic *t* statistics are in parentheses. Dependent variable is 1 if the individual has a pension in the final year and is 0 otherwise.

results indicate the difference in net outcomes associated with having a pension on the original job. They suggest that, in both the SIPP and the PSID data, a person who moved from a pension job was only about 12 percent more likely to have obtained a new job that offered a pension.[18]

The comparable differences in table 4.1 were 22 percent (35.8 percent minus 13.8 percent) in the SIPP data and 16 percent (53.2 percent minus 37 percent) in the PSID data. Since the multivariate results suggest that movers from pension jobs have marginal effects of 12 percent relative to movers from nonpension jobs in finding new employment with pensions, the gap calculated in the previous few paragraphs would be, if anything, understated.

Association of Defined Contribution Plans with Mobility

For the SIPP panel data, the fraction of pension-covered workers whose initial pension is a defined benefit plan, the most common type of primary plan, is reported in the last row of the middle section of table 4.1.[19] In that data set, almost two-thirds of the primary plans for those initially covered in 1984 are defined benefit.

Table 4.6 further examines descriptive data from the SIPP. It disaggregates the results for pension-covered workers according to whether the coverage was by a defined benefit or defined contribution plan. Because the SIPP question sequence on plan type is atypical, two sets of results are included for defined contribution plans. Respondents were first asked, "Is _'s (basic) retirement plan a profit-sharing plan?" If they responded no, they were then asked, "Are the retirement benefits of _'s (basic) pension plan determined by years of service and pay or by the amount of contributions to the plan?" In the first set of defined contribution results, respondents are classified as having defined contribution plans if they answered yes to the initial question or chose the second alternative of the second question. Another set of defined contribution results is limited to only those respondents who had nonprofit-sharing defined contribution plans (i.e., those who responded no to the first question and chose the second alternative to the second question). These plans comprise only about 10 percent of the total plans, and hence should be relatively uncontaminated by misclassified defined benefit plans.

According to the SIPP data in table 4.6, workers with defined contribution plans are slightly more mobile than workers with defined benefit plans (6.2 percent or 6.9 percent versus 6.0 percent), but the differences are not significant. In terms of wages, the patterns of workers covered by defined benefit and nonprofit-sharing defined contribution plans are very similar, with movers suffering around a 10 percent wage loss in both cases. For workers under profit-sharing plans, the pattern is slightly different. Movers from these plans appear to come from lower levels in the wage distribution and do not suffer any wage loss in their new jobs. However, this group has the lowest mobility rate of all (5.9 percent for the profit-sharing plans only), indicating that just a small number of these workers found better alternative jobs.

Table 4.6 Wages, Pensions, and Mobility by Pension Status and Plan Type in the Initial Survey: SIPP

Pension type	Stayers		Movers	
Defined benefit pension in 1984 job				
Percent movers	a	a	6.0%	(1,126)
Mean wage in 1984	$11.95	(960)	$11.94	(58)
Mean wage in 1985	$11.94	(960)	$10.81	(58)
Percent with 1985 pension	a	a	42.9%	(63)
Defined contribution pension in 1984 job (including profit-sharing plans)				
Percent movers	a	a	6.2%	(627)
Mean wage in 1984	$11.73	(530)	$9.94	(30)
Mean wage in 1985	$11.82	(530)	$9.96	(30)
Percent with 1985 pension	a	a	21.9%	(32)
Defined contribution pension in 1984 job (excluding profit-sharing plans)				
Percent movers	a	a	6.9%	(174)
Mean wage in 1984	$11.53	(149)	$12.03	(8)
Mean wage in 1985	$11.44	(149)	$10.70	(8)
Percent with 1985 pension	a	a	22.2%	(9)

NOTES: Figures in parentheses are numbers of observations. Wages are indexed to 1984 dollars by the Index of Average Hourly Earnings (1989 *Economic Report of the President*, table B-44) and are included in the means only if valid wage observations are available in both years. Means are geometric means (i.e., antilogs of mean log wages). Wages less than $1 or greater than $50 are excluded from the analysis.
a. Not applicable.

Table 4.7 presents estimates of the relationship of plan type to mobility in the context of a probit equation formulated with SIPP data.

Table 4.7 Pension Effects from Mobility Equations Using SIPP Panel Data

Pension explanatory variables	Estimate (*t* statistic)					
	Equation 1		Equation 2		Equation 3	
Pension coverage	-0.090	(6.50)				
Defined benefit pension			-0.092	(5.87)	-0.092	(5.86)
Defined contribution pension			-0.087	(4.93)		
Profit-sharing pension					-0.090	(4.51)
Nonprofit-sharing pension					-0.080	(2.70)
Log-likelihood	-748.34		-748.31		-748.25	
Number of observations	2,545		2,545		2,545	

NOTES: The dependent variable is job separation. Entries are marginal responses in probit estimates. Numbers in parentheses are absolute values of asymptotic *t* statistics. Additional explanatory variables are age, education, experience, years until expected retirement, with binary variables for manufacturing, white collar, management, union status, firm size over 100, race, marital status, children under 18, home ownership, and residence in a Standard Metropolitan Statistical Area (SMSA).

Analogous results are presented in table 4.8 for the retrospective SCF data. The first column in each table gives the marginal effect of the pension coverage variable in a probit equation that also relates mobility to personal and job characteristics.[20] The job characteristics in the SIPP data refer to the initial job; in the SCF data, they refer to the longest job. In the SIPP data, union status and work experience are as of the end of the period covered by the third interview, while the other variables pertain to the beginning of the period covered by the fourth interview.

Table 4.8 Pension Effects from Mobility Equations Using SCF Retrospective Data

| | Estimate (*t* statistic) | | | |
Pension explanatory variables	Equation 1		Equation 2	
Pension coverage	-0.57	(10.90)		
Defined benefit pension			-0.61	(10.23)
Defined contribution pension			-0.69	(3.77)
Log-likelihood	-242.21		-239.85	
Number of observations	581		581	

NOTES: The dependent variable is job separation. Table entries are estimated marginal effects of a probit model. Numbers in parentheses are absolute values of asymptotic *t*-statistics.

The marginal effect of a simple pension coverage variable is highly significant in this equation. Indeed, the pension variable has by far the most powerful impact on mobility behavior of any of the variables considered. In the case of the SIPP data, evaluated at the means, pensions are associated with a 9 percentage point reduction in one-year mobility rates, which is two-thirds of the pension/nonpension mobility differential. For the five-year mobility rate in the SCF data, pension coverage is associated with a 57 percentage point difference in mobility.

The second columns of data in tables 4.7 and 4.8 report marginal effects from an equation that separates the pension variable according to whether the pension is defined benefit or defined contribution. To the extent that the impact of pensions on mobility operates through backloading, defined contribution plans should not exhibit any effect since they are not backloaded (see table 2.4). Nevertheless, in both data sets, the coefficients of the defined benefit and defined contribution variables are each highly significant and are almost identical in magnitude, and a formal test of the hypothesis that they are equal is not rejected at almost any level of significance.

The third column appears only in table 4.7, which is for the SIPP data. That column refers to results separating the defined contribution variable into profit-sharing plans and nonprofit-sharing plans, as discussed previously. Again, there is little evidence of a strong differential effect of defined benefit and defined contribution plans on mobility. These results are not what one would expect if backloading were an important factor in the differential mobility rates from pension versus nonpension jobs, and they raise further questions about the cause of any relationship found between pension backloading and mobility.

Overview of Descriptive Results

Cross tabs and simple multivariate analyses from three surveys point to the conclusions that wages are higher on jobs offering pensions than on jobs that do not offer pensions, that compensation differences are even wider, and that there are systematic relationships between pension coverage, compensation level, and mobility. Movers from pension jobs experience large losses in wages and larger losses in compensation. In contrast, movers from nonpension jobs experience wage gains in two of the three surveys and a small wage loss in the third, with compensation gains in all three surveys. Contrary to the predictions of models in which pension backloading accounts for the difference in mobility between workers who are covered by pensions and those who are not, defined contribution plans are just as likely to be associated with reduced mobility as are defined benefit plans. Thus, the results suggest both that compensation is higher on pension-covered jobs and that it is the higher compensation, rather than pension backloading, that is associated with lower mobility from these jobs.

NOTES

1. When we analyzed the panel data from the 1986 SCF in a report to the U.S. Department of Labor (Gustman and Steinmeier 1990), we found the attrition bias from the survey to be severe and systematic, so as to affect the reliability of the resulting analysis. The panel from the 1989 SCF was not available at the time of writing this book.

2. Analysis with the SIPP data indicated that the subsample for which the reason for turnover was available was not representative of the full sample. See our report to the U.S. Labor Department (Gustman and Steinmeier 1990).

3. The data analysis in this book is confined to males in order to avoid the complicating effects of career interruptions.

4. Mobility is considered to have occurred for an individual if there was a separation from the initial job and a new job was started by the beginning of the last period covered in the survey. In the SCF, this occurred if the individual's current job (or last job, if not currently employed) began after 1978. In the SIPP, it occurred if, in the intervening interviews, the individual clearly indicated that he had stopped working at one job and had started another. (The SIPP provides job numbers, but these are unreliable indicators as to whether or not jobs in two different interviews were the same.) In the PSID, mobility occurred if the current job as of 1989 began after 1984 or if the individual reported that he separated from his previous employer in any of the intervening surveys. For all of the surveys, individuals who did not hold jobs in the initial year were dropped from the sample.

5. Farber (1993) finds that there is some evidence that job displacement was different between the late and the early 1980s. In the later period, displacement was more likely to affect those in nonmanufacturing and to affect older workers with less tenure.

6. In an attempt to provide a comparable analysis with the PSID and SIPP data, we also estimated the mobility model for a two-year period with the PSID data. However, with fewer observations on mobility, the estimating procedure does not converge for the shorter period.

7. Thus, the SCF and PSID data will be used to calculate mobility over a five-year period. Given the limited number of observations in the SCF and the PSID and the availability of pension information in the PSID only for 1984 and 1989, it is not practical to analyze mobility for either survey over the shorter, one-year period analyzed with the SIPP data. On the other hand, the SIPP data are not available for the longer period.

8. Another potential source of differences in outcomes is attrition. Attrition equations are presented for the panel data from the SIPP and PSID in the appendix to this chapter. Major differences in attrition are not apparent. However, there is no attrition in the retrospective survey, although there is censoring of some data in the base period, which is discussed in this chapter.

9. As the discussion in chapter 3 indicates, previous studies of mobility that estimated pension backloading and related backloading to mobility also did not have direct measures of pension backloading available. These studies had to match pension incentives to individuals on the basis of industry and other characteristics reported by the respondent.

10. Further descriptive statistics for the SIPP and PSID are in appendix tables 4.1 and 4.2. Because not all initial jobs are observed in the retrospective SCF, a corresponding table cannot be calculated for that data set.

11. The full results underlying table 4.2 in the text are reported in appendix table 4.3.

12. To the extent that additional compensation reflects a reward for additional effort, the disutility of the additional effort should be netted out of current compensation.

13. Allen, Clark, and McDermed (1991) attempt to standardize for the opportunities facing different workers on alternative jobs by including the current wage and human capital indicators in the mobility equation.

14. Given the censoring of some wage observations in the initial period for the retrospective SCF data, a simple estimate of a wage equation is not presented.

15. The F statistic for the hypothesis that the coefficients of the two equations are equal is 1.88, which is almost exactly the same as the 5 percent critical value of 1.89 for $F(20,628)$. The F statistic for excluding the two interaction terms in the combined equation is 0.09.

16. In the retrospective data, wage changes are observable only for movers; even then, there is some censoring of observations for those who moved during the period. Accordingly, in evaluating these descriptive numbers, it must be remembered that the data are not fully representative and are not adjusted for selectivity bias and censoring, as are the compensation estimates made while fitting the full econometric models in chapter 6.

17. The full multivariate results are reported in appendix table 4.4.

18. Referring now only to the SIPP data, the pension figures for the new job are limited to individuals who report participation in a pension plan at the time of the 1985 survey. Including those who are not participating because they "have not worked for the employer long enough" raises to 20.6 percent the share of movers from nonpension jobs who gained pensions in their new jobs and reduces to 55.8 percent the proportion of movers from pension jobs who lost their pensions.

19. Again, the PSID data do not indicate plan type for the age range covered by the study.

20. The full results for the first equations of both tables are presented in appendix table 4.3. The other equations use the same explanatory variables, except that the pension variable is split as indicated.

Appendix to Chapter 4
Part A: Descriptive Statistics

Appendix Table 4.1 Descriptive Statistics for SIPP Movers and Stayers

	Estimate (Observations)			
	No pension in 1984		Pension in 1984	
Variable	Stayers	Movers	Stayers	Movers
Wages and pensions				
1984 log wage	2.164 (654)	2.044 (133)	2.474 (1,490)	2.418 (88)
1985 log wage	2.182 (654)	2.108 (133)	2.476 (1,490)	2.353 (88)
1985 pension	0.0 (803)	13.8 (160)	100.0 (1,646)	35.8 (95)
1984 defined benefit plan	a	a	64.3 (1,646)	63.6 (107)
1984 defined contribution plan	a	a	35.7 (1,646)	36.4 (107)
1984 multiple plans	a	a	8.8 (1,646)	9.3 (107)
1985 defined benefit plan	a	54.5 (22)	a	73.5 (34)
1985 defined contribution plan	a	45.5 (22)	a	26.5 (34)
1985 multiple plans	a	13.6 (22)	a	5.9 (34)
Personal characteristics				
Black	7.5 (803)	6.7 (195)	7.0 (1,646)	2.8 (107)
Age	38.4 (803)	37.6 (195)	39.8 (1,646)	39.3 (107)
Experience	18.8 (773)	17.7 (186)	20.4 (1,608)	18.8 (101)
Expected retirement age	64.2 (264)	64.9 (53)	62.3 (757)	63.3 (41)
Education	12.7 (802)	12.7 (195)	13.3 (1,646)	13.3 (107)
Married	77.8 (803)	75.9 (195)	85.7 (1,646)	89.7 (107)
Children	60.8 (803)	63.1 (195)	66.6 (1,646)	67.3 (107)

Job characteristics

Firm size: < 25 employees	37.4	(803)	39.5	(195)	8.1	(1,646)	9.3	(107)
25-99	20.9	(803)	21.0	(195)	9.7	(1,646)	20.6	(107)
100+	41.7	(803)	39.5	(195)	82.3	(1,646)	70.1	(107)
Union	11.9	(731)	8.9	(168)	35.1	(1,591)	35.0	(100)
SMSA	52.6	(803)	60.0	(195)	54.6	(1,646)	52.3	(107)
Blue collar	49.6	(803)	57.4	(195)	45.0	(1,646)	41.1	(107)
White collar	10.6	(803)	11.8	(195)	11.4	(1,646)	13.1	(107)
Management & professional	39.9	(803)	30.8	(195)	43.6	(1,646)	45.8	(107)
Mining	1.1	(803)	0.5	(195)	1.4	(1,642)	3.8	(106)
Construction	9.5	(803)	20.0	(195)	5.2	(1,642)	17.9	(106)
Durable manufacturing	18.6	(803)	20.0	(195)	29.4	(1,642)	17.9	(106)
Nondurable manufacturing	9.7	(803)	10.3	(195)	16.9	(1,642)	17.0	(106)
Transportation, communication, and public utilities	9.6	(803)	8.2	(195)	13.9	(1,642)	8.5	(106)
Wholesale trade	8.1	(803)	3.6	(195)	7.4	(1,642)	8.5	(106)
Retail trade	15.8	(803)	15.9	(195)	8.7	(1,642)	9.4	(106)
Finance, insurance & real estate	6.1	(803)	4.6	(195)	5.6	(1,642)	4.7	(106)
Services	21.5	(803)	16.9	(195)	11.5	(1,642)	12.3	(106)

NOTE: Number of observations for each cell is in parentheses.
a. Not applicable or no observation.

Appendix Table 4.2 Descriptive Statistics for PSID Movers and Stayers

	Estimate (Observations)			
	No pension in 1984		Pension in 1984	
Variable	Stayers	Movers	Stayers	Movers
Wages and pensions				
1984 wage	2.218 (59)	2.236 (53)	2.559 (221)	2.472 (78)
1989 wage	2.298 (59)	2.211 (53)	2.572 (221)	2.36 (78)
1989 pension	31.6 (79)	37.0 (108)	85.6 (263)	53.2 (126)
Personal characteristics				
Experience	18.2 (77)	18.8 (102)	18.9 (261)	17.4 (125)
Age	37.3 (79)	37.9 (108)	38.5 (263)	37.7 (126)
Education	12.7 (78)	13.1 (108)	13.1 (263)	14.1 (125)
Black	7.6 (79)	1.9 (108)	5.3 (263)	4.8 (126)
Married	82.3 (79)	78.7 (108)	92.0 (263)	87.3 (126)
Children	70.9 (79)	74.1 (108)	75.7 (263)	73.8 (126)
Home ownership	79.7 (79)	73.1 (108)	88.2 (263)	73.8 (126)
Spouse employed	59.5 (79)	48.1 (108)	60.8 (263)	52.4 (126)
Job characteristics				
Manufacturing	24.1 (79)	20.4 (108)	48.3 (263)	36.5 (126)
Blue collar	46.8 (79)	46.3 (108)	52.5 (263)	35.7 (126)
White collar	16.5 (79)	12.0 (108)	6.1 (263)	16.7 (126)
Management & professional	36.7 (79)	41.7 (108)	41.4 (263)	47.6 (126)

Union	10.1 (79)	4.6 (108)	36.3 (262)	16.7 (126)
SMSA	45.6 (79)	55.1 (107)	51.5 (262)	56.3 (126)

NOTE: Number of observations for each cell is in parentheses.

Appendix Table 4.3 Probit Estimates of Reduced Form Mobility Equations

| | Marginal effects (*t* statistic) | | |
	1978-1983 SCF	1984-1985 SIPP	1984-1989 PSID
Variable			
Personal characteristics			
Years of experience	0.02 (2.46)	0.00[b] (1.21)	0.00[b] (0.08)
Years of education	0.01 (1.17)	0.00[b] (0.17)	0.03 (2.33)
Years until expected retirement	0.01 (1.71)	0.00[b] (1.44)	a
Black	-0.18 (1.87)	-0.07 (2.15)	-0.14 (1.31)
Age	-0.01 (0.79)	0.00[b] (1.22)	0.01 (0.22)
Married	-0.02 (0.26)	0.01 (0.64)	-0.02 (0.21)
Children under 18	0.07 (1.25)	0.01 (0.83)	0.07 (1.06)
Home ownership	-0.23 (4.03)	-0.05 (0.27)	-0.21 (3.45)
Spouse employed	0.00[b] (0.01)	a	-0.05 (1.03)
Job characteristics			
Manufacturing	0.07 (1.32)	-0.01 (0.71)	-0.04 (0.82)
White collar	0.10 (1.14)	0.00[b] (0.00)	0.05 (0.69)
Management/professional	0.01 (0.11)	-0.02 (0.96)	-0.05 (0.84)
Union	0.00[b] (0.06)	0.00[b] (0.13)	-0.19 (2.91)
Firm size > 100 employees	0.03 (0.53)	-0.01 (0.98)	a
Pension coverage	-0.57 (10.90)	-0.09 (6.50)	-0.21 (4.24)

SMSA	0.01 (0.25)	0.01 (0.99)	0.02 (0.54)
Log-likelihood	-242.21	-748.34	-340.39
Number of observations	581	2,545	561

NOTE: Absolute values of asymtotic t statistics are in parentheses. Dependent variable is 1 if the individual separates and is 0 otherwise.

a. Variable is omitted from this equation.

b. Coefficient is less than 0.005 in absolute value.

90

Appendix Table 4.4 Probit Estimates of Final Pension Status for Those Who Change Jobs

Variable	Marginal effects (t statistic)			
	1984-1985 SIPP		1984-1989 PSID	
Personal characteristics				
Years of experience	0.00[b]	(0.38)	-0.01	(0.57)
Years of education	0.01	(0.44)	0.00	(0.77)
Black	-0.11	(0.58)	-0.15	(0.71)
Age	0.00[b]	(0.11)	0.01	(0.44)
Married	0.08	(0.81)	-0.01	(0.07)
Children under 18	0.00[b]	(0.06)	0.13	(1.20)
Home ownership	0.06	(0.89)	0.13	(1.46)
Spouse employed	a		-0.13	(1.63)
Characteristics of initial job				
Manufacturing	0.08	(1.24)	0.11	(1.35)
White collar	0.18	(1.68)	0.04	(0.34)
Management/professional	0.17	(2.04)	0.05	(0.56)
Union	0.26	(3.11)	0.07	(0.55)
Firm size > 100 employees	-0.03	(0.40)	a	
Pension	0.12	(1.79)	0.12	(1.61)
SMSA	0.02	(0.35)	-0.03	(0.40)
Log-likelihood	-108.74		-145.65	
Number of observations	232		226	

NOTE: Absolute values of asymptotic t statistics are in parentheses. Dependent variable is 1 if the individual has a pension after separation and is 0 otherwise.
a. Variable is omitted from this equation.
b. Coefficient is less than 0.005 in absolute value.

Appendix to Chapter 4
Part B: Analysis of Attrition

Appendix Table 4.5 Probit Equations Analyzing Attrition Among Pension-Covered Workers

| | Marginal effects (t statistic) | | | |
| | 1984-1985 SIPP | | 1984-1989 PSID | |
Variable	Pension-covered workers	Nonpensioned workers	Pension-covered workers	Nonpensioned workers
Personal characteristics				
Years of experience	-0.001 (0.30)	-0.002 (0.78)	0.001 (0.08)	0.000[b] (0.04)
Years of education	0.005 (1.27)	-0.003 (0.56)	0.011 (1.04)	0.001 (0.65)
Years until expected retirement	-0.001 (0.23)	0.002 (0.25)	a	a
Black	0.037 (1.07)	-0.081 (1.52)	-0.024 (0.31)	0.102 (0.74)
Age	0.003 (0.77)	0.002 (0.26)	-0.001 (0.16)	0.001 (0.06)
Married	-0.030 (0.98)	0.021 (0.58)	0.026 (0.38)	0.049 (0.47)
Children under 18	0.003 (0.12)	-0.046 (1.54)	-0.099 (2.38)	-0.014 (0.16)
Home ownership	-0.040 (1.58)	-0.038 (1.38)	-0.030 (0.61)	-0.012 (0.17)
Spouse employment	a	a	-0.014 (0.35)	-0.053 (0.88)

Job characteristics

Log wage	a		a		-0.006	(1.30)	0.000[b] (0.08)
Manufacturing	0.013	(0.71)	-0.037	(1.29)	0.027	(0.70)	0.034 (0.59)
White collar	0.011	(0.34)	0.106	(2.59)	-0.078	(0.93)	-0.080 (0.83)
Management/professional	-0.041	(1.54)	-0.009	(0.27)	-0.037	(0.68)	-0.158 (1.97)
Union	-0.007	(0.32)	0.026	(0.62)	0.038	(0.83)	a
Firm size > 100 employees	0.042	(1.68)	0.025	(0.94)	a		a
SMSA	0.021	(1.15)	0.023	(0.89)	0.038	(1.01)	-0.029 (0.51)
Log-likelihood	-1,081.04		-578.7		-132.94		-41.93
Number of observations	2,134		1,140		382		148

NOTE: Absolute values of asymptotic t statistics are in parentheses. Dependent variable is 1 for attrition and is 0 otherwise.
a. Variable is omitted from this equation.
b. Coefficient is less than 0.005 in absolute value.

5
Econometric Specification
of the Mobility
and Compensation Equations

Having discussed descriptive results relating to pensions, wages, and mobility, we now turn to the specification of our econometric mobility model. The model will be estimated in chapters 6 and 7. Three versions of the model are considered.

The first version, estimated for the Survey of Income and Program Participation (SIPP) and the Panel Study of Income Dynamics (PSID), starts with two equations for compensation in the current and next best jobs. It adds a mobility equation in which mobility is a function of the difference in compensation in these two jobs, with compensation in both cases being measured over the remainder of the individual's working life. The model allows for the fact that we do not observe compensation in the next best job unless the individual moves.

The second version of the model, estimated for the 1983 Survey of Consumer Finances (SCF), adds a selection equation since we do not always observe the individual's starting job in that data set. After estimating these models, we are able to simulate the effects of the compensation differential between the two jobs. Further, for pension-covered workers, we can separate the part of the differential due to backloading and simulate its effect on mobility. This will permit us to gauge the importance of backloading as an impediment to mobility.

The third form of the model relaxes a constraint that is implicit in the first two versions. In this case, the compensation differential in the mobility equation is split into two parts: one due to pension backloading and the second due to other causes of compensation differentials between the present and next best job. By allowing the coefficients on separate variables measuring backloading and other compensation differentials to be estimated freely within the mobility equation, we create a specification test for the model. If the model were completely specified to incorporate all dimensions of behavior important to the turnover decision, one would expect identical coefficients in the mobility equation for the effect of the two parts of the compensation differential. That is, in the absence of specification error, the effect on the prospects for mobility from a dollar's worth of compensation should be the same whether it comes from pension backloading or from some other source.[1] That model is estimated in chapter 7 with data from the SIPP and the PSID. The PSID data are also used to estimate the latter version of the model with quits rather than total job separations as the outcome, implicitly assuming that layoffs are random.

The Basic Model

In the basic version of the model, mobility is indicated by the latent variable M^*,

(5.1) $$M^* = \alpha\,(\ln C_c - \ln C_a) + X_1\beta_1 + \varepsilon_1.$$

If mobility has occurred, M^* is positive; otherwise, it is negative. C_c is compensation in the current job, and C_a is compensation in the alternative job, with all compensation measured in dollars per hour until retirement. The expectation is that α will be negative, as higher relative compensation on the current job discourages mobility. X_1 is a vector of explanatory variables, β_1 is a vector of coefficients, and ε_1 is a normally distributed error term.

Compensation in the current job (C_c) is specified with the following equation:

(5.2) $$\ln C_c = X_2\beta_2 + \varepsilon_2$$

where X_2 is a vector of explanatory variables, β_2 is a vector of coefficients, and ε_2 is a normally distributed error term. Compensation in the alternative job (C_a), which is observed only if the individual moves, is given in a similar equation:

(5.3) $$\ln C_a = X_3\beta_3 + \varepsilon_3$$

where X_3 is another set of explanatory variables, β_3 is a vector of coefficients, and ε_3 is another normally distributed error term. Note that X_3, in theory, cannot contain job characteristics of the new job, since these are only observed if an individual moves. In practice, the explanatory variables in X_2 and X_3 are the same.

The compensation levels in each job include both the value of wages and pensions. C_c and C_a are calculated as the average hourly amount of wages plus pension accrual to each year of service from the start of the period until retirement. Here, retirement is the earlier of the individual's expected retirement age or the age of normal retirement in the individual's pension plan (if the worker has one). The rationale is that if an individual will ever find it advantageous to switch jobs before the normal retirement age, it will be as soon as possible, given the positive effects of tenure on wages and the typical backloading of pension benefits toward the end of the job. Hence, the appropriate comparison is the total compensation in the two jobs from the current date until the normal retirement age in the plan or until the individual's expected retirement date, if that is earlier.

To facilitate estimation, the term for C_a is substituted from equation (5.3) into (5.1):

$$(5.4) \qquad M^* = \alpha\,(\ln C_c - X_3\beta_3) + X_1\beta_1 + \varepsilon_1^*.$$

In this equation, $\varepsilon_1^* = \varepsilon_1 - \alpha\varepsilon_3$.

Equations (5.2), (5.3), and (5.4) and the correlation among the error terms in the three equations are estimated jointly by maximum likelihood. The maximum likelihood procedures are analogous for estimating the basic model, as specified in equations (5.2) to (5.4), and for estimating the alternative versions of the model presented in the next section. The details of the likelihood function and its estimation are deferred to an appendix.

The Basic Model as Modified for Censoring of Wage Observations in the Initial Period

In the retrospective SCF, the 1978 job is not observed for some individuals because of the manner in which the job history was collected. C_c cannot be calculated for those individuals, and another equation is required to describe whether or not the 1978 job, and hence C_c, is observed.[2] This selection equation uses the latent variable I^*:

$$(5.5) \qquad I^* = X_4\beta_4 + \varepsilon_4$$

where the 1978 job is observed if I^* is positive and is not observed otherwise. X_4 is a vector of explanatory variables, β_4 is a vector of coefficients, and ε_4 is a normally distributed error term. For (5.5) to be valid as a selection equation, X must include all the explanatory variables in both the mobility equation (5.1) and the compensation equations (5.2) and (5.3).[3]

The fact that we cannot always observe C_c means that we must also substitute in for C_c in equation (5.4):

$$(5.6) \qquad M^* = a\,(X_2\beta_2 - X_3\beta_3) + X_1\beta_1 + \varepsilon_1^*.$$

In this equation, $\varepsilon_1^* = \varepsilon_1 + \alpha(\varepsilon_2 - \varepsilon_3)$.

The Mobility Equation with Pension Backloading and Other Compensation Differences as Separate Independent Variables

The mobility equation to be estimated with the third version of the model is given by

$$(5.7) \qquad M^* = \alpha_1\,(\ln C_c - \ln C_n) + \alpha_2\,(\ln C_n - \ln C_a) + X_1\beta_1 + \varepsilon_1$$

where, again, M^* is an indicator variable that is positive if the worker changes jobs during the period and negative otherwise. C_c and C_n are the compensation in the current job and the non-backloaded part of compensation in the current job, respectively, and C_a is compensation in the alternative job, with all compensation measured in dollars per hour until retirement. The first two terms on the right-hand side of the equation are the backloaded and nonbackloaded parts of the compensation premium, with α_1 and α_2 as their coefficients. As before, X_1 is a vector of explanatory variables, and ε_1 is a normally distributed error term.

The equations for $\ln C_a$ and $\ln C_c$ are as specified in equations (5.2) and (5.3). To estimate the mobility equation, following the procedures outlined earlier, we first substitute from equation (5.3).

$$(5.8) \qquad M^* = \alpha_1 \left(\ln C_c - \ln C_n \right) + \alpha_2 \left(\ln C_n - X_3 \beta_3 \right) + X_1 \beta_1 + \varepsilon_1^*.$$

Once again, $\varepsilon_1^* = \varepsilon_1 - \alpha_2 \varepsilon_3$. Since the error structure of this model is exactly the same as in the first model, the set of equations (5.2), (5.3), and (5.8) can be estimated by the same maximum likelihood procedures.

Having specified the econometric model, we now turn to its estimation. Chapter 6 discusses the estimation of the model in which mobility is a function of the overall compensation differential between the initial job and the next best alternative.

Appendix to Chapter 5
Derivation of the Likelihood Function

In this appendix, we will derive the likelihood function for the second model. The likelihood functions for the other models are similar, except for the lack of the selection equation and the integrals related to that equation.

To facilitate the presentation of the estimation procedure, a slight change in notation will be convenient. We have denoted the compound error term from the mobility equation (5.6) to be ε_1^*. To simplify notation, let ε_i^* be equal to ε_i for the remaining equations (5.2, 5.3, and 5.5), and let the correlation matrix for the ε_i^* as Σ^*. The correlation matrix Σ for the original ε_i s can be derived from Σ^* by straightforward calculations, if desired.

It is assumed that the error terms ε_i are statistically independent of the explanatory variables in the X vectors for the various equations. If so, the likelihood function for the model is simply the product of the probability expressions for the individual observations. The form of these probability expressions depends on which compensation values are observed. There are three possible cases, as follows. First, consider the situation where the 1978 job is included in the employment history and where the individual did change jobs during the period, so that both compensation values are observed. The probability density of this observation is given as

$$(5.9) \qquad PR_j = \int_{-\hat{M}-\hat{I}}^{\infty} \int^{\infty} f(\hat{\varepsilon}^*) \, d\varepsilon_4^* d\varepsilon_1^*$$

where $\hat{M}$ and $\hat{I}$ are the deterministic parts of equations (5.5) and (5.6), respectively, and j indexes the individual. $\hat{\varepsilon}^*$ is a vector of the four ε_i^* s, with ε_2^* and ε_3^* taking on the values solved from equations (5.2) and (5.3) using the observed compensation values and the values of the explanatory variables. This probability expression integrates the probability density $f(\hat{\varepsilon}^*)$ of the error terms over the region where the mobility indicator is positive ($M^* > 0$) and the selection indicator is positive ($I^* > 0$).

The second case arises if the 1978 job is not observed and the individual changed jobs during the period. This implies that C_c, the compensation value for the 1978 current job, is not observed but that C_a, the compensation value for the alternative job, is observed. The probability density for the observation for this case is

$$(5.10) \qquad PR_j = \int_{-\hat{M}}^{\infty} \int_{-\infty}^{-\hat{I}} f(\varepsilon_1^*, \varepsilon_3^*, \varepsilon_4^*)\, d\varepsilon_4^* d\varepsilon_1^* .$$

This equation is different in two respects from the expression in the previous example. First, the limits in the second integral are changed to reflect the lack of observation for the 1978 job. Also, the probability density $f(\varepsilon_1^*, \varepsilon_3^*, \varepsilon_4^*)$ has been integrated out with respect to ε_2^*, the residual in the equation determining the unobserved compensation value in 1978.

The third case occurs if the 1978 job is observed and the individual remained in the job over the period. Here, C_c is observed, but C_a is not. The probability density of the observation is

$$(5.11) \qquad PR_j = \int_{-\infty}^{-\hat{M}} \int_{-\hat{I}}^{\infty} f(\varepsilon_1^*, \varepsilon_2^*, \varepsilon_4^*)\, d\varepsilon_4^* d\varepsilon_1^*.$$

This is the same kind of integral as in the previous case, except for obvious changes in the integration limits and the substitution of ε_2^*, which can be computed in this case, for ε_3^*, which cannot.

There is one data problem that is relevant to the estimation procedure. The data necessary to construct wage information for a particular job are missing in about 15 percent of the cases. An ideal solution would be to use separate selection equations for these cases, but doing so would increase the dimensionality of the cumulative normal to be evaluated by two dimensions and would make the estimation procedure computationally much more difficult. Instead, we make the assumption that the process inducing the omissions is statistically independent to the explanatory variables and error terms in the various equations. The likelihood function can then be integrated out with respect to the error terms associated with missing wages. This would cause ε_2^* or ε_3^*, depending on which wage is missing, to be dropped from the appropriate probability density formula for the observation. For example, suppose that the 1978 job is observed and a job change did occur, but that the 1978 wage is missing. The probability density for the individual in this case would be

$$(5.12) \qquad PR_j = \int_{-\hat{M}}^{\infty} \int_{-\hat{I}}^{\infty} f(\varepsilon_1^*, \varepsilon_3^*, \varepsilon_4^*)\, d\varepsilon_4^* d\varepsilon_1^* .$$

If instead the 1978 job is not observed, a job change did occur, and the alternative job wage is missing, the probability density would be

(5.13)
$$PR_j = \int\limits_{-\hat{M}}^{\infty} \int\limits_{-\infty}^{-\hat{I}} f(\varepsilon_1^*, \varepsilon_4^*)\, d\varepsilon_4^* d\varepsilon_1^* \ .$$

Having constructed the log-likelihood from the sum of the logs of the probability expressions PR_j of the individual observations, maximum likelihood estimates are obtained by maximizing this function with respect to the parameters in the model. These parameters include α, the ßs, and the elements of the correlation matrix Σ^*. The maximization technique is a scoring algorithm with a linear search along the indicated direction in combination with the Berndt-Hall-Hall-Hausman routine for evaluating the expected second derivative matrix (Berndt et al. 1974). This algorithm also provides asymptotic standard errors for the estimated parameters of the model.

NOTES

1. It would be unreasonable to expect precise agreement between the two estimated coefficients. Important factors have been omitted, such as the risk associated with each form of compensation, or associated differences in effort that go unmeasured. Nevertheless, large discrepancies in the estimated coefficients should point to major misspecifications that cause the error term in the mobility equation to be correlated with pension backloading or with the remainder of the compensation differential.

2. Note, however, that even though the retrospective SCF missed some 1978 jobs (which necessitated the selection equation), it specifically asked about previous pension-covered jobs, so that if the question were answered, the data should include all 1978 jobs with pensions.

3. As noted, C_a is not observed for individuals who remained in their 1978 jobs at least through 1983. Normally, this would require another selection equation, but the selection equation in this case is the mobility equation (5.1), which is already included in the model. Hence, an additional equation is not required.

6
Econometric Estimates
with Mobility a Function
of Compensation Differentials

The distinguishing feature of the first two versions of the mobility model developed in chapter 5 is that, in the mobility equation, there is only a single measure of the compensation differential between those workers on pension-covered jobs and those on jobs not offering pensions. That is, in the estimation of the mobility equation itself, the compensation differential is not decomposed into components attributable to backloading and to other factors. That estimation is postponed until chapter 7. Instead, the models in this chapter estimate the effect of the total compensation differential on mobility. To isolate the effect of backloading, we separate that part of the compensation differential and infer its effects on compensation from the coefficient on the compensation differential in the mobility equation. This coefficient is simply the α in equation (5.4).

We begin by fitting the first version of the model, which is suitable to panel data, to results from the Survey of Income and Program Participation (SIPP) and the Panel Study of Income Dynamics (PSID). Then we fit the second version of the model to the retrospective Survey of Consumer Finances (SCF). Once these models are estimated and we have parameter estimates for mobility and compensation equations, we turn to simulation analysis. These simulations help to answer two questions. First, can the compensation differentials between current and best alternative jobs explain very much of the difference in mobility between pension-covered and noncovered workers, or can the difference be explained primarily by the other variables in the mobility equation? Second, how much does pension backloading affect the difference in mobility rates between these two groups? In these simulations, we maintain the underlying assumption that a one-dollar differential in compensation, whatever its source, should have the same effect on mobility.

The empirical results in this chapter indicate that it is not the pension capital loss from mobility that is primarily responsible for the negative relationship between pension coverage and mobility. Those who are covered by pensions receive a higher level of compensation on their jobs than do those without pensions, and at least a part of this appears to be a compensation premium over and above what these workers could obtain elsewhere. It is this premium, rather than the pension loss from moving, that accounts for the large difference in mobility between pension-covered workers and those who are not covered by a pension on their initial jobs.

Model Based on SIPP Data Estimates

This section estimates the first version of the pension-mobility model described in chapter 5, using the data from the SIPP.[1] Job changes are measured over the one-year period between the fourth and seventh interviews in the SIPP. As before, a job change is considered to have occurred when the individual leaves the position held at the beginning of the period and takes one with a different employer.

Unlike the SCF, the SIPP does not have available an employer-provided pension plan description. Instead, SIPP individuals are matched with employer plan descriptions from the SCF with the same industry, occupation, and union status. The wage profile of the SIPP worker is applied to the detailed plan description for each of the SCF plans in the industry/occupation/union status cell, and the pension amounts for the SIPP worker are taken as the weighted average of the pension amounts for the pensions in the cell. The matching process uses SIC three-digit industries and three occupations; if there are no pension-provider observations in that cell, cells are collapsed to two-digit or one-digit industries, as required, until a filled cell is found. In no cases are union plans used to impute nonunion plans, or vice versa. This procedure allows the pension calculations to take account of the wide differences in plans across industries, occupations, and union status.

In the SIPP estimates, the mobility equation is identified by excluding the pension variable. With regard to the two compensation equations, identification is achieved by excluding the household variables.

Compensation is calculated as the average per-hour amount of wages plus increases in pension values between the initial year and the earlier of the individual's expected date of retirement from full-time work or the normal retirement age specified in the pension plan (if the employee had one). If the individual did not provide an expected retirement age, the terminal date for the compensation calculations is taken to be the normal retirement age in the pension plan for employees with pensions and age 65 for employees without pensions. A real wage profile is created by using the observed wage and extrapolating to dates before and after on the basis of the estimated coefficients of the experience and tenure variables in the wage regressions reported in chapter 4. This is converted to a nominal profile by taking into account the general growth of nominal wages. Pension values are calculated by applying the resulting wage profile to the individual's own pension. All compensation amounts reported in this section are discounted to 1984 and expressed in 1984 dollars.

Table 6.1 presents estimates for this model. The estimates for the mobility latent variable are in the left two columns of data, and the estimates for the compensation in the initial and alternative jobs are in the remaining columns. For the mobility equation, only the measures of the compensation premium and home ownership are significant at standard levels. Home ownership lowers estimated mobility by 3.3 percentage points, and a 10 percent larger compensation difference between the initial and alternative job is estimated to decrease mobility by 2.9 percentage points (10 percent of 0.293).

The equation for compensation in the initial job exhibits coefficients that are consistent with expectations. Compensation is significantly and positively related to pension coverage, white-collar jobs, management and professional employment, union and large-firm employment, level of education, and work in a Standard Metropolitan Statistical Area (SMSA). Compensation is significantly lower for Blacks. In the alternative compensation equation, coefficients are significant for schooling and location in an SMSA, with some other estimated coefficients near significance. Pension coverage in the job held in the base period is associated with a compensation premium of about 22 percent, the difference between the coefficients on the pension coverage variables in the 1984 compensation equation and in the alternative job compensation equation (0.343 minus 0.126).

Table 6.1 Estimates of the Model with Mobility Determined by a Single Measure of the Compensation Premium Based on 1984-85 Data from the SIPP

Model component	Mobility equation		Compensation in 1984 job	Compensation in alternative job
	Marginal effect	(t statistic)	Estimate (t statistic)	Estimate (t statistic)
Constant			1.430 (14.80)	0.939 (1.43)
Compensation premium (α)	-0.293	(2.58)	a	a
Pension coverage	a		0.343 (17.80)	0.126 (0.74)
Manufacturing	0.004	(0.17)	0.029 (1.45)	-0.006 (0.09)
White collar	0.024	(0.58)	0.073 (2.42)	-0.008 (0.07)
Management/professional	0.011	(0.37)	0.233 (10.28)	0.157 (1.57)
Union status	0.023	(0.63)	0.117 (4.79)	0.034 (0.32)
Firm size > 100	0.018	(0.65)	0.058 (3.03)	-0.038 (0.43)
Years of experience	-0.002	(0.75)	0.000[b] (0.17)	0.002 (0.26)
Years until retirement	-0.001	(0.32)	-0.003 (1.37)	0.010 (1.03)
Age	0.002	(0.91)	a	a
Education	0.002	(0.45)	0.058 (16.66)	0.067 (4.19)
Race (Black)	0.059	(0.63)	-0.190 (4.88)	-0.551 (1.85)
Married	0.009	(0.61)	a	a
Children under 18	0.009	(0.75)	a	a
Home ownership	-0.033	(2.06)	a	a

SMSA	-0.024	(0.98)	0.061	(3.40)	0.177	(2.43)
Standard deviation of error terms	1.000	--	0.425	(92.53)	0.477	(7.62)
Correlation matrix of error terms	1.000		0.707		0.409	(1.03)
			1.000	--	0.355	(4.33)
					1.000	--

Log-likelihood   -2,304.57

Number of observations   2,545

NOTES: Numbers in parentheses are absolute values of asymptotic t statistics. See text for descriptions of the dependent variables. The job characteristics in the alternative job equation refer to the characteristics in the initial job, not to the characteristics of the alternative job.
a. Variable is omitted from this equation.
b. Coefficient is less than 0.0005 in absolute value.

To interpret the correlations reported in the table, it is important to remember that they refer to the ε^* terms, that is, the composite errors after substituting for the alternative wage into equation (5.4). The correlations for the original error terms can be found by using the standard formulas for variances, covariances, and correlations. The resulting estimated correlation matrix is as follows:[2]

Mobility equation	Compensation in 1984 job	Compensation in alternative job
1.000	0.413	-0.414
	1.000	0.355
		1.000

Thus, although the estimated value of $p(\varepsilon_1^*, \varepsilon_2)$ is strongly positive at 0.707, the estimated value of $p(\varepsilon_1, \varepsilon_2)$, which is the correlation between the probability of mobility for unobserved reasons and the level of compensation offered on the initial job for unobserved reasons, is reduced to 0.413. The fact that the error terms in these two equations are positively correlated follows the pattern of many of the observed variables that are entered in both equations. For example, being in a large firm raises initial compensation, and it also increases the probability of mobility, *holding the compensation premium constant*.

Simulations

Simulations with the model allow us to do two things. First, we can see how well the model fits the data, both for the whole sample and for subgroups of particular interest. Second, the simulations can help us to ascertain the degree to which the lower mobility of pension-covered workers is due to pension backloading and the degree to which it is due to the greater pay and benefits on pension-covered jobs.

These simulations are performed as follows. For each individual, the nonstochastic part of equation (5.4) is calculated as $\hat{M}$. If compensation in either the current or alternative job is observed, it is possible to calculate ε_2 and/or ε_3 from equations (5.2) and (5.3), given the coefficient estimates and the values for the explanatory variables. It is then possible to calculate the probability that the individual would have changed jobs in the one-year interval.[3]

Consider now how well the model predicts the actual mobility rate, both for the sample as a whole and for important subgroups within the sample. The simulations relevant for this question are presented in table 6.2. The first column of data in the table gives the observed mobility rate for the group in question during the one-year period, while the middle column gives the mobility rate simulated by the model using the explanatory variables for that particular group.

Table 6.2 Model Validation Simulations Based on 1984-85 Data from the SIPP

Group	Sample mobility (percent)	Simulated mobility (percent)	Number of observations
Full sample	9.73	9.71	2,545
Individuals with pensions	5.71	5.71	1,678
Individuals without pensions	17.35	17.27	867
Union members	6.91	7.16	692
Not union members	10.76	10.64	1,853

The simulations capture the disparities in mobility rates among very different groups rather well. For example, the actual one-year job mobility for the sample is about 11.6 percentage points higher for individuals without pensions than for individuals with pensions, and the magnitude of this differential is reflected in the simulated mobility rates. This is particularly encouraging because pensions are not an explicit explanatory variable in the mobility equation in the model. A similar result holds, though less dramatically, when the mobility rates are compared between union members and others. In this case, the mobility rate among union members is 3.9 percentage points lower than for individuals not in unions, and, again, the magnitude of this differential is reflected in the simulation results. Thus, the simulation model does appear to do a good job of predicting differences in the mobility rates of various groups, even of some groups not explicitly represented in the mobility equation itself.

Next we would like to examine the role of pensions in affecting job mobility. In order to assess the importance of backloading for mobility, it is necessary to consider the magnitude of the backloading as well as the impact per dollar. This is done in table 6.3, which presents the results of several simulations using sample members with pensions. The results in the first column of data simply repeat the base simulation reported in table 6.2. (The numbers do not match for various subgroups, since table 6.2 represents all members of a subgroup and table 6.3 represents only members of the subgroup with pensions.) In the second column, one part of the compensation premium is deleted. For instance, in the first part of the table, the simulations exclude the backloaded part of the compensation premium and calculate the mobility rate that would occur if only the nonbackloaded part of the premium were present.[4]

Table 6.3 Simulations of Effects of Backloading and Other Changes in Compensation on Mobility Based on 1984-85 Data from the SIPP

Group	Original mobility rate (percent)	Postchange mobility rate (percent)	Number of observations
Effects of eliminating pension backloading on			
All individuals with pensions	5.71	6.39	1,678
46-50 year-olds	4.35	5.35	359
Union members	5.70	6.49	590
Not union members	5.72	6.34	1,088
Effects of dropping pension compensation entirely			
All individuals with pensions	5.71	10.38	1,678
Effects of higher compensation in pension jobs, as measured by compensation equation estimates			
All individuals with pensions	5.71	14.39	1,678

The first four rows of the table analyze the effects of the backloading component of compensation for each of four populations of pension-covered workers. Recall that the basic mobility rates for pension-covered and noncovered workers were 5.7 percent and 17.4 percent, respectively, in the descriptive data of table 6.2. The comparison between the two data columns in the first row of table 6.3 suggests that backloading accounts for about two-thirds of one percentage point of mobility, or about 6 percent of the total difference in mobility rates between pensioned workers and nonpensioned workers. The impact of backloading is somewhat larger for older workers. When the same exercise is done in the second row for the 359 pension-covered workers in the 46-50 age range, excluding backloading raises the mobility rate from 4.35 percent to 5.35 percent, a full percentage point. This is half again as large as the effect for the full age range, but it is still small relative to the gap in mobility rates between pensioned and nonpensioned workers. As seen in the third and fourth rows, the estimated effects of pension backloading on mobility for subgroups categorized by union status are also below 1 percentage point.

The fifth row of data in the table excludes the pension entirely from the premium. As might be expected on the basis of the relative sizes of pension values and backloading reported in table 2.2, the total effect of the pension, at almost 4.7 percentage points, is substantially larger than the effect of backloading alone. This is to say that most of the effect of pensions on mobility occurs because of the basic value of the pensions themselves, not because they are backloaded.

The final row in the table reports the effect of eliminating the entire compensation premium associated with pension jobs. To estimate the value of the premium, the effects of pensions in the two compensation equations are compared. As reported in table 6.1, the coefficient of the pension variable in the current compensation equation is 0.343, while the corresponding coefficient in the alternative compensation equation is 0.126 (with t statistics of 17.80 and 0.74, respectively). These estimates imply that pensions are associated with an increase of 0.217 in the difference between log compensations in the current job and the alternative job, where the difference is the compensation premium. The simulation excludes this amount from the premium, with the result that mobility would increase by about 8.7 percentage points. This is about three-fourths of the total differential between the mobility rates of pensioned and nonpensioned workers in table 6.2. In comparison with the much smaller reduction from backloading alone, it suggests that the nonbackloaded part of the premium has more responsibility for the relatively low mobility rates among pension-covered workers. To put it another way, restructuring pensions to be perfectly portable would increase the mobility of pension-covered workers very little.

Model Based on Data from the PSID Estimates

Table 6.4 presents the estimates of the mobility model for data from the PSID. In the PSID, as with the SIPP, it is necessary to calculate pension amounts based on a match with the employer pension plan data from the SCF.

The results of this estimation are broadly consistent with the results from the SIPP estimation in the previous section. In the mobility equation, the compensation premium is one of two significant variables, along with home ownership as the other. The result implies that a 10 percent gain in the compensation premium would decrease mobility by 6.4 percentage points. Once again, the amount of compensation in the 1984 job is positively and significantly influenced by pension coverage, manufacturing employment, managerial and professional work, union employment, higher levels of schooling, and work in an SMSA. Blacks again receive significantly lower compensation. Consistent with earlier findings, schooling is the dominant variable in the compensation equation in alternative employment. Finally, the effect of pension coverage in the initial job on the difference between the compensation in that job and in the alternative job (30 percent) is a bit above the compensation difference found with the SIPP data (22 percent).[5]

Analysis of Quits

In this section, the PSID provides the only data allowing analysis that distinguishes quits from layoffs. Appendix table 6.1 presents the results of the estimation of the three-equation model in which turnover is defined as quits rather than as separations. These results are analogous to those in table 6.4 and indicate that, in the PSID data, there are no significant differences in findings when quits are substituted for separations. In particular, a very similar coefficient estimate is obtained both for the marginal effect of the compensation premium (at −0.552 with a t statistic of 2.34, versus −0.648 with a t statistic of 2.29). The other key result is the coefficient on the pension measure in the equations for compensation on the 1984 job and on the alternative job. The pension coefficients in the two equations are .276 with a t statistic of 7.61 and .013, with a t statistic of 0.09. The implication is that having a

Table 6.4 Estimates of the Model with Mobility Determined by a Single Measure of the Compensation Premium Based on 1984-89 Data from the PSID

Model component	Mobility equation		Compensation in 1984 job		Compensation in alternative job	
	Marginal effect	(t statistic)	Estimate	(t statistic)	Estimate	(t statistic)
Constant			2.150	(60.28)	2.092	(10.40)
Compensation premium (α)	-0.648	(2.29)	a		a	
Pension coverage	a		0.276	(7.58)	-0.026	(0.14)
Manufacturing	0.111	(1.14)	0.069	(1.82)	0.191	(1.52)
White collar	-0.063	(0.29)	0.073	(1.08)	0.189	(0.59)
Management/professional	-0.016	(0.12)	0.240	(5.21)	0.243	(1.27)
Union status	0.102	(0.58)	0.202	(3.83)	-0.156	(0.89)
Years of experience	-0.002	(0.19)	0.000	(0.16)	-0.008	(0.67)
Age	0.007	(0.68)	a		a	
Education	-0.022	(0.79)	0.071	(7.94)	0.125	(3.44)
Race (Black)	-0.070	(0.23)	-0.264	(3.40)	-0.291	(0.65)
Married	0.000b	(0.00)	a		a	
Children under 18	-0.010	(0.16)	a		a	
Home ownership	-0.186	(2.93)	a		a	
Spouse employment	-0.025	(0.49)	a		a	
SMSA	0.043	(0.46)	0.087	(2.54)	0.086	(0.65)

Table 6.4 (continued)

Model component	Mobility equation		Compensation in 1984 job		Compensation in alternative job	
	Marginal effect	(t statistic)	Estimate	(t statistic)	Estimate	(t statistic)
Standard deviation of error terms			0.341	(32.78)	0.519	(6.27)
Correlation matrix of error terms	1.000	--	0.531	(2.00)	0.479	(1.34)
			1.000	--	0.322	(2.58)
					1.000	--
Log-likelihood			-531.58			
Number of observations			474			

NOTE: Numbers in parentheses are absolute values of asymptotic t statistics. See text for descriptions of the dependent variables. The job characteristics in the alternative compensation equation refer to the characteristics in the initial job, not to the characteristics of the alternative job. Firm size is unavailable in the PSID, and years until retirement is omitted because it is reported only for those age 45 or older.
a. Variable is omitted from the equation.
b. Coefficient is less than 0.0005 in absolute value.

pension on the current job raises compensation relative to the next best opportunity by about twenty-five percent.

Simulations

Model validation simulations for the PSID data are presented in table 6.5. In this case, the period for mobility is five years. Again the simulated mobility rates capture the disparities in outcomes among the groups. There is, however, more of an underprediction of mobility for those without pensions than was evident with the SIPP data.

Table 6.5 Model Validation Simulations Based on 1984-89 Data from the PSID

Group	Sample mobility (percent)	Simulated mobility (percent)	Number of observations
Full sample	41.8	40.9	474
Individuals with pensions	32.1	33.3	331
Individuals without pensions	64.2	58.4	143
Union members	23.9	23.7	119
Not union members	48.0	46.9	355

Consider now the simulations examining the effects of pensions on mobility, decomposing the effects into those associated with backloading and with the compensation premium on pension-covered jobs. These simulations are presented in table 6.6. Again, the results in the first column of data are for the base simulations using observed compensation in the mobility equation, while the results in the second column are based on simulations that exclude some part of the compensation premium.

As shown in the last row of the table, the total effect of the compensation differences associated with holding a pension-covered job is a reduction in mobility from 54.1 percent to 33.3 percent. Thus, the compensation premium can account for most of the difference in mobility rates between pensioned and nonpensioned workers (32.4 percent versus 57.8 percent, from table 4.1). However, the portion of the difference that is due to pension backloading is only 3.2 percentage points (36.5 percent minus 33.3 percent), which is small compared to the effect of the full value of the pension, or of the compensation premium on pension-covered jobs. For 46-to-50-year-olds, pension backloading *per se* has almost twice the effect that backloading does for the full sample, but it is still not the major reason that workers in pension jobs have lower turnover rates than workers in nonpension jobs.

Table 6.6 Simulations of Effects of Backloading and Other Changes in Compensation on Mobility Based on 1984-89 Data from the PSID

Group	Original mobility rate (percent)	Postchange mobility rate (percent)	Number of observations
Effects of eliminating pension backloading			
All individuals with pensions	33.3	36.5	331
46-50 year-olds	27.5	33.0	50
Union members	22.1	25.5	108
Not union members	39.1	42.2	223
Effects of dropping pension compensation entirely			
All individuals with pensions	33.3	43.2	331
Effects of higher compensation in pension jobs, as measured by compensation equation estimates			
All individuals with pensions	33.3	54.1	331

Model Estimates Based on Retrospective Data from the SCF

This section presents estimates of the mobility model using retrospective SCF data. As explained in chapter 5, the econometric methodology is slightly modified from that developed for true panel data. All versions of the model must deal with the lack of information on the opportunity wage for those who stayed in the same job over the period of observation. In addition, when estimating the model with retrospective data, there is a lack of information on the base period job for some of those who moved. The modification in methodology addresses the problem of data that is missing for that reason.

Mobility is calculated on the basis of a job change in the five-year period preceding the survey, that is, from 1978 to 1983. Basic descriptive information on job-changing behavior over this period has been presented in chapter 4. Once again, these data suggest that mobility is significantly lower among pension-covered workers.

Several of the employment-related measures, including industry, occupation, union status, and firm size, which are used as explanatory variables in the model, refer to the longest-held job. This is necessitated because information on these variables for the 1978 job is not available for everyone in the sample.[6] Since the variables for the longest-held job refer to a major labor force experience, they should be fairly indicative of the 1978 job as well. The nature of the data set imposes another temporal mismatch, which involves several of the household variables, including marital status, the presence of children, home ownership, and whether the wife was employed. The values of these variables pertain to 1983, the year in which the data set was collected, although again it would be preferable to use values for 1978.

Before moving to the estimates for the model, one problem with measuring pension values and pension incentives retrospectively in the SCF should be noted. The pension-provider data in the survey are available only for jobs held in 1983, not in 1978. Even then there are some individuals who claim eligibility for pensions but for whom pension-provider records are absent in the data set, and there are other individuals for whom pension-provider records are available but are seriously deficient in some critical regard. No pension-provider information at all is available for the small group of individuals who indicated having a pension in 1978 but who changed jobs before 1983. Therefore, missing pension data are imputed using techniques described in the first section of this chapter. In total, imputations are made for about two-fifths (41 percent) of the pension values. Twenty-three percent are imputed on the basis of three-digit industry cells and 7 percent and 9 percent on the basis of two-digit and one-digit industry cells, respectively, all using the correct occupation category and union status. The remaining 2 percent are imputed by collapsing cells across occupations, with 1 percent using three-digit industry and 1 percent using two-digit industry cells.

Table 6.7 presents the results of the maximum likelihood estimator of the second version of the full model, as described in chapter 5.[7] With this procedure, the maximum of the likelihood function is achieved at the boundary defined by the requirement that the estimated correlation matrix for the error terms (Σ^*) be positive definite. The standard errors

Table 6.7 Estimates of the Model With Mobility Determined by a Single Measure of the Compensation Premium Based on 1978-83 Retrospective Data from the SCF

Model component	Mobility equation		Compensation in 1978 job		Compensation in alternative job		1978 job selection equation	
	Marginal effect	(t stat)	Estimate	(t stat)	Estimate	(t stat)	Estimate	(t stat)
Constant			1.248	(4.63)	0.786	(0.72)	-1.164	(0.46)
Compensation premium (α)	-0.83	(2.92)	d		d		d	
Pension coverage[a]	d		0.392	(5.02)	-0.362	(1.59)	d	
Manufacturing[b]	0.12	(0.86)	0.074	(1.42)	0.055	(0.39)	-0.034	(0.14)
White collar[b]	-0.17	(0.78)	0.064	(0.78)	0.454	(1.85)	-0.500	(1.39)
Management/professional[b]	0.06	(0.47)	0.226	(3.59)	0.135	(0.97)	0.185	(0.64)
Union[b]	-0.15	(0.98)	0.110	(2.10)	0.304	(1.70)	-0.087	(0.32)
Firm size > 100[b]	d		0.120	(2.14)	0.019	(0.19)	-0.279	(1.27)
Years of experience[a]	0.02	(1.29)	-0.004	(0.93)	0.000[e]	(0.02)	-0.028	(0.95)
Years until expected retirement[a]	0.01	(0.45)	-0.006	(1.35)	0.001	(0.07)	0.001	(0.03)
Age[a]	-0.01	(0.56)	d		d		0.037	(0.70)
Years of education[a]	-0.01	(0.48)	0.087	(8.07)	0.122	(4.16)	-0.005	(0.11)
Race (Black)[c]	0.08	(0.23)	-0.186	(2.12)	-0.513	(1.37)	0.287	(0.74)
Married[c]	0.08	(0.64)	d		d		0.010	(0.02)

Children under 18[c]	0.05 (0.62)	d	d	0.028 (0.10)
Home ownership[c]	-0.33 (3.90)	d	d	0.600 (2.34)
Wife employed[c]	-0.03 (0.44)	d	d	0.054 (0.22)
SMSA[c]	-0.08 (0.64)	0.109 (2.32)	0.228 (1.86)	0.170 (0.80)
Standard deviation of error terms		0.41 (26.91)	0.57 (9.00)	
Correlation matrix of error terms	1.00 --			
	0.14 (1.01)	1.00 --		
	0.61 (3.14)	0.45 (3.47)	1.00 --	
	-0.95 --	0.03 (0.11)	-0.34 (0.11)	1.00 --
Log-likelihood	-597.99			
Number of observations	558			

NOTE: Figures in parentheses are absolute values of asymptotic t statistics.

a. Measured in 1978.

b. Job held longest.

c. Measured in 1983.

d. Variable is omitted from this equation.

e. Coefficient is less than 0.0005 in absolute value.

in table 6.7 are, therefore, the result of a constrained estimation. All of the correlation parameters, except the correlation between the error terms in the 1978 job selection and mobility equations, are treated as free, with this remaining correlation calculated as the value necessary to just meet the positive semidefiniteness requirement. As a consequence of this procedure, no standard error is estimated for this correlation, as indicated in the table, and the estimated standard errors for the remaining correlations should be interpreted with this constraint in mind.

In the mobility equation, only two of the variables are significant at standard levels. As with the SIPP, one of these is home ownership and the other is the compensation premium, which is of particular interest to this study. Once again, the impact of the compensation premium variable on mobility is by far the largest. The estimates imply that a 10 percent gain in this variable would result in an 8.3 percentage point decrease in job mobility. This effect is about one-third larger than the effect found over the comparable five-year period using the PSID data. Among the remaining variables, union membership has the expected negative effect on mobility and is sizable, but not significant.

In the 1978 job compensation equation, quite a few of the coefficients are significant, and the significant coefficients all have the expected signs. Compensation is positively and significantly related to pension eligibility, management/professional occupations, union membership, firm size, education, and SMSA residency, and is significantly lower for Blacks. For compensation in an alternate job, education once again has a clearly significant impact, in the positive direction. Other variables close to significance include union membership, SMSA residency, and white-collar occupations.

The one major difference between the results based on panel data from the SIPP and PSID on the one hand, and the retrospective SCF data on the other, is in the magnitude of the effect of pension coverage on the current and alternative job. With data from all three surveys the pension measure is significant only in the equation for compensation on the current job, and the estimated difference in pension coefficients between the current and next best job is only about half as large in the SIPP and PSID data as in the SCF data.

The 1978 job selection equation suggests that average compensation values are not much affected by the inclusion or exclusion of the 1978 job from the job history. Only one variable, home ownership, is significant in this equation, and this variable is not a determinant of compensation. Nor are the correlations between the error term in the job selection equation and the error terms of the two compensation equations significant. The lack of correlation implies that the presence or absence of the 1978 job from the job history does not greatly influence compensation values through unobserved factors contained in the error terms.

The other correlation estimates contain few surprises. The estimated correlation matrix of the original error terms, calculated along the same lines as in note 2, is the following:

Mobility equation	Compensation in 1978 job	Compensation in alternative job	1978 job selection equation
1.00	0.34	-0.06	-0.27
	1.00	0.45	0.03
		1.00	-0.34
			1.00

The correlation pattern among the first three error terms is similar to that of the SIPP estimates, except that here the correlation between ε_1 and ε_3 is negligible. The correlations in the last column imply that the error term in the 1978 job selection equation is negatively associated both with the error term in the mobility equation and with the error term in the alternative job compensation equation. The negative correlations are not surprising, since the 1978 job will not be missing in the job history unless the individual changed jobs in the interim, and a low alternative wage makes it less likely that the individual will have changed jobs. The error terms in the two compensation equations are moderately correlated at 0.45, and the correlation is significant.

Model Validation

Table 6.8 compares the actual mobility rate with the rate predicted by the simulations, for the sample as a whole and for the indicated subgroups within the sample.[8] Consider how well the simulations capture the disparities in mobility rates among the different groups. The actual five-year job mobility for individuals without pensions is about 47 percentage points higher than for individuals with pensions, and this entire differential is reflected in the simulated mobility rates. Once more, we note that this is so despite the fact that pensions are not included as an explanatory variable in the mobility equation in the model. Differences in mobility between union members and nonunion members are also predicted well. In this case, the mobility rate among union members is about 12 percentage points lower than for individuals not in unions, and again the whole differential is reflected in the simulation results.

Table 6.8 Model Validation Simulations Based on 1978-83 Retrospective Data from the SCF

Group	Sample mobility (percent)	Simulated mobility (percent)	Number of observations
Full sample	28.0	29.8	558
Individuals with pensions	8.8	10.1	331
Individuals without pensions	55.9	58.4	227
Union members	20.1	21.2	204
Not union members	32.5	34.9	354

Unlike the simulations based on estimates from the SIPP and PSID data, the SCF simulations in table 6.8 are consistently one to two percentage points higher than the actual data. The reasons for this are not entirely clear but may be related to the likelihood of maximization occurring along a boundary. In any case, this overestimation is quite small when compared to the large-scale differences in mobility rates among different groups, and it does not seem to have affected the ability of the model to predict these differences among groups successfully.

Simulations

We turn again to the role of pensions in affecting job mobility. Table 6.9 presents the relevant simulations. The top portion of the table examines the effect of pension backloading on mobility, both for the whole sample of individuals covered by pensions and for the specific subgroups considered previously. For those with pensions, the simulated five-year mobility rate with the observed compensation is 10.3

percent. Eliminating backloading, the mobility rate rises only to 11.6 percent. This small effect reflects the fact that backloading in the sample for table 6.7 amounts to only about 3 percent of compensation (as calculated according to note 4) between 1978 and the expected retirement age.

Table 6.9 Simulations of Effects of Backloading and Other Changes in Compensation on Mobility, Based on 1978-83 Retrospective Data from the SCF

Group	Original mobility rate (percent)	Postchange mobility rate (percent)	Number of observations
Effects of eliminating pension backloading			
All individuals with pensions	10.3	11.6	286
46-50 year-olds	9.8	12.3	54
Union members	11.8	13.3	143
Not union members	8.9	9.8	143
Effects of dropping pension compensation entirely			
All individuals with pensions	10.3	15.7	286
Effects of higher compensation in pension jobs, as measured by compensation equation estimates			
All individuals with pensions	10.3	52.3	286

Again, the effect for the older individuals in the group, who are closer to the retirement ages specified in the plans and for whom the incentive impacts of backloading should be greater, is indeed larger. However, the increase in these workers' mobility rates is only about 2.5 percentage points over the five-year period. This is still very small when compared to the nearly 50 percentage point difference in the mobility rates of those with and without pensions (table 6.8). The effect of backloading is also not very large among either union or non-union members as a group, as indicated by the next two rows in the table.

When we simulate the effect of eliminating pensions, with no compensating adjustments in wages or other benefits, thereby removing the effects of the pension backloading as well as of the pension value itself, the impact on mobility is over four times as large as that of simply eliminating backloading. Nevertheless, the effect is still relatively small compared to the total differential in mobility between those with and without pensions.

In the last line of the table, we analyze the effects of changing the compensation premium measure in the mobility equation by the amount the estimated pension coefficients indicate in the compensation equations. The estimates of the compensation equations in table 6.7 suggest that a pension in the 1978 job reduces $\ln C_a$, the alternative job compensation, by 0.362 and increases $\ln C_c$, the compensation in that job, by 0.392. Hence, the effect of a pension on the difference between $\ln C_c$ and $\ln C_a$, which is the compensation premium associated with current employment on a pension-covered job, is 0.754. (Again, this is about twice the difference found with the SIPP and PSID data.) To simulate the effect of this change, the value of $\hat{M}$ in the simulations is increased by 0.754 times the coefficient of the compensation premium variable. The results of this simulation are indeed striking. Job mobility would increase to 52.3 percent were the compensation premium abolished, which is very close to the measured mobility for those without pensions.

This outcome is sensitive to the estimated difference in pension coefficients in the two compensation equations, and these coefficients, particularly in the alternative job equation, are not precisely estimated. The estimated difference of 0.754 is comparable to the actual difference of 0.568 in the mean log compensation between pensioned and nonpensioned workers in the sample for table 6.7. Further, even if the difference and its associated impact on job mobility were cut in half, it would be very difficult to avoid the conclusion that mobility in pension jobs is low mostly because these jobs pay a high compensation premium. Only a relatively minor role appears to be played by the backloading of pensions, whereby benefits are concentrated toward the end of the job.

Other Issues in Specification

In the model specification, the assumptions have generally tended to bias the results toward showing larger effects of pension backloading than in fact exist. First, the pension variable is omitted completely from the mobility equation. This omission forces the large pension effect in the reduced form equation to work entirely through the compensation gain measure, likely biasing the coefficient upward. The bias would occur if pensions do have a direct effect on mobility or if they are proxies for other variables that should enter the mobility equation. Second, the model has treated a dollar's worth of expected pension benefits as having the same value as a dollar of earnings. In fact, most people would argue that, because of the greater uncertainty regarding the eventual receipt of pensions, these benefits should be valued at some lesser amount. This would mean that even more of the effect of pensions on mobility should be attributed to the wage premium and even less to pensions and backloading than our results would indicate. Finally, we have not included the possibility that individuals in pension-covered jobs have a lower inherent propensity to change jobs. The impact of backloading would be overstated to the extent that mobility actually due to heterogeneity is instead attributed to pension-related factors.[9] Hence, we conclude that our estimates of the small impacts of pension backloading on mobility are, if anything, likely to be an overstatement of the true effects.

Summary and Conclusions

This chapter has shown that a model consisting of a mobility equation and equations for compensation on the current job and compensation on the next best job may be used to determine the likely effects on mobility from pension backloading and from compensation differentials between the current and next best job. The model assumes that all sources of compensation differences have the same effect on workers' mobility decisions. Accordingly, mobility has been expressed as a function of the compensation difference between the current job and the next best alternative. In the process of estimating the mobility equation, we have allowed for the fact that compensation in the next best employment is not observed for stayers.

Econometric estimates have been obtained from three different data sets. These estimates indicate that compensation differences vary directly with pension coverage. Pension-covered workers receive higher future compensation on their current jobs due to backloading of their pensions, due to the contribution of the pension to compensation, and because the pension benefit is not offset by lower wages, but instead is accompanied by higher wages.

The examination of compensation on current and alternative employment suggests that, on pension-covered jobs, the compensation premium constitutes a much more important fraction of the loss from job termination than does backloading of pension benefits. Simulations with the mobility equations confirm that it is not backloading, but the wage premium that explains the large difference in mobility between workers with pension-covered and noncovered jobs. These differences in mobility have been broken down into components reflecting the effects of pension backloading and the other sources of compensation differences for employment with and without pensions. In each case, the findings in tables 6.3, 6.6, and 6.9 suggest that pension backloading accounts for no more than about 10 percent of the difference in mobility between those workers on pension-covered jobs and those holding jobs that do not offer pensions.

NOTES

1. This section incorporates material from our article (Gustman and Steinmeier 1993b), which, in turn, is based on a report to the U.S. Department of Labor (Gustman and Steinmeier 1990, under contract No. J-9-P-8-0098.)

2. Recalling that the variance of ε_1^* is normalized to unity, and using the standard formula for correlation ($\rho_{12} = \sigma_{12}/\sigma_1\sigma_2$), the covariance matrix of the composite error terms (the ε_i^*) can be calculated as:

1.000	0.300	0.195
	0.181	0.072
		0.228

Since the relation between ε_1 and ε_1^* is $\varepsilon_1 = \varepsilon_1^* + \alpha\varepsilon_3$, $\text{Var}(\varepsilon_1) = \text{Var}(\varepsilon_1^*) + 2\alpha\text{Cov}(\varepsilon_1^*, \varepsilon_3) + \alpha^2\text{Var}(\varepsilon_3)$, $\text{Cov}(\varepsilon_1, \varepsilon_2) = \text{Cov}(\varepsilon_1^*, \varepsilon_2) + \alpha\text{Cov}(\varepsilon_2, \varepsilon_3)$, and $\text{Cov}(\varepsilon_1, \varepsilon_3) = \text{Cov}(\varepsilon_1^*, \varepsilon_3) + \alpha\text{Var}(\varepsilon_3)$. Evaluating these formulas yields the following covariance matrix of the original error terms:

1.005	0.176	-0.198
	0.181	0.072
		0.228

Applying the standard formula for correlations gives the correlation matrix in the text.

3. This probability is

$$PR_j = \int_{-\hat{M}}^{\infty} f(\varepsilon_1^* | \varepsilon_2, \varepsilon_3)\, d\varepsilon_1^*$$

which is the integral of the probability density for ε_1^* above the value of $-\hat{M}$. If either the compensation in the current or alternative job is unobserved so that ε_2 or ε_3 cannot be calculated, the density function f is integrated out with respect to those error terms. The simulated mobility rate for the sample is the sample weighted average of the mobility probabilities for the individuals in the sample. In the results presented in table 6.2, the simulated mobility rates are weighted averages, but runs with unweighted averages gave very close to the same results.

4. The effect of pension backloading is computed in accordance with the discussion in chapter 2. For each individual in a pension covered job, we calculate the value of the pension rights should the individual remain until retirement. We then make a calculation for a defined contribution plan of the same value at retirement, which serves as the counterfactual plan with the elimination of the backloading that typically occurs in a defined benefit plan.

5. The correlation matrix among the original error terms, calculated along the lines of note 2, is:

1.000	0.260	-0.407
	1.000	0.322
		1.000

These figures are approximately the same as for the SIPP estimates, with the exception of the correlation between ε_1 and ε_2, which is only about two-thirds as large.

6. The SCF did not collect a full work history for all respondents. In particular, information is reported for the current and longest-held job, which for some individuals who moved after 1978 may not be the job held in 1978.

7. Some additional details of the estimation are as follows:

Agricultural employment and self-employment are screened on the basis of the individual's longest-held job, since information on these characteristics is not always available for the 1978 job.

If the individual was unemployed in 1983, he or she was considered to be a mover if the previous job began after 1978, and a stayer if the previous job began before 1978. This effectively measures mobility as the taking of a new job and not as the separation (which may or may not be temporary) from an old job.

The general growth rate of nominal wages used in the calculations is the 30-year average from 1953-83, and the discount factor is equal to the general growth rate of nominal wages.

By the construction of the data set, all 1978 jobs with pensions are observed. Hence, the pension coefficient in the 1978 job selection equation has an implied value of $+\infty$ and is not estimated.

Also note that in the mobility equation, an additional year of experience is accompanied by another year of age and by a reduction in the number of years until expected retirement. All three coefficients must be considered to determine the total effect on mobility of becoming another year older, which is close to nil.

8. Simulations with the retrospective SCF involve slightly different calculations than the simulations with the panel data. For each individual, the nonstochastic parts of equations (5.5) and (5.6) in Chapter 5 are calculated as $\hat{I}$ and $\hat{M}$, respectively. Also, if compensation in either the current or alternative job is observed, it is possible to calculate the values ε_2 and/or ε_3 from equations (5.2) and (5.3). If the 1978 job is observed, it is possible to calculate the probability that the individual would have changed jobs in the one-year interval as

$$PR_j = \int_{-\hat{M}}^{\infty} f\left(\varepsilon_1^* \mid \varepsilon_2, \varepsilon_3, \varepsilon_4 > -\hat{I}\right) d\varepsilon_1^*$$

If the 1978 job is not observed, the probability is

$$PR_j = \int_{-\hat{M}}^{\infty} f\,(\varepsilon_1^* | \varepsilon_2, \varepsilon_3, \varepsilon_4 < -\hat{I})\, d\varepsilon_1^* \quad .$$

In both cases, the probability is the integral of the conditional probability density for ε_1^* above the value of $-\hat{M}$. Note that if the 1978 job involved a pension, $\hat{I}$ is infinitely positive, since the SCF specifically asked about previous pension jobs. As before, if either the compensation in the current or alternative job is unobserved so that ε_2 or ε_3 cannot be calculated, the density function f is integrated out with respect to those error terms. The simulated mobility rate for the sample is the average of the mobility probabilities for the individuals in the sample.

9. The effects of self selection of stayers into pension covered jobs remains in doubt. We have included in the mobility equation those observables which Allen, Clark and McDermed (1991) find are correlated with selection into pension covered jobs. Moreover, Allen, Clark and McDermed conclude that unobservables do not play an important role in the selection process.

Appendix to Chapter 6: PSID Results with Quits Only as the Dependent Variable and with a Single Measure of the Compensation Premium

Appendix Table 6.1 PSID Model Estimates with Quits Only as the Dependent Variable

Model component	Mobility equation		Compensation in 1984 job		Compensation in alternative job	
	Marginal effect	(t stat)	Estimate	(t stat)	Estimate	(t stat)
Constant			2.150[a]	(59.61)	2.181[a]	(18.75)
Compensation premium (α)	-0.552	(2.34)	[a]		[a]	
Pension coverage	[a]		0.276	(7.61)	0.013	(0.09)
Manufacturing	-0.169	(1.95)	0.069	(1.83)	0.227	(1.80)
White collar	-0.155	(0.71)	0.074	(1.08)	0.205	(0.60)
Management/professional	0.031	(0.24)	0.241	(5.16)	0.244	(1.29)
Union status	-0.024	(0.14)	0.202	(3.87)	-0.097	(0.58)
Years of experience	-0.000[b]	(0.02)	0.000[b]	(0.16)	-0.006	(0.55)
Age	0.001	(0.06)	[a]		[a]	
Education	-0.011	(0.43)	0.071	(7.90)	0.122	(3.65)
Race (Black)	-0.240	(0.74)	-0.264	(3.47)	-0.310	(0.66)
Married	0.056	(0.58)	[a]		[a]	
Children under 18	-0.001	(0.01)	[a]		[a]	
Home ownership	-0.175	(2.56)	[a]		[a]	

Appendix Table 6.1 (continued)

Model component	Mobility equation		Compensation in 1984 job		Compensation in alternative job	
	Marginal effect	(t stat)	Estimate	(t stat)	Estimate	(t stat)
Spouse employment	0.020	(0.40)	a		a	
SMSA	0.028	(0.31)	0.087	(2.54)	0.073	(0.55)
Standard deviation of error terms			0.341	(33.12)	0.505	(14.49)
Correlation matrix of error terms	1.00	--	0.574	(2.29)	0.317	(2.16)
			1.00	--	0.346	(4.27)
					1.00	--
Log-likelihood			-433.8			
Number of observations			474			

NOTES: Numbers in parentheses are absolute values of asymptotic *t* statistics. See text for descriptions of the dependent variables. The job characteristics in the alternative compensation equation refer to characteristics in the initial job, not to the characteristics of the alternative job.
a. Variable is omitted from this equation.
b. Coefficient is less than 0.0005 in absolute value.

7
Econometric Estimates with Separate Backloading and Compensation Premium Variables

A further modification of the mobility model is analyzed in this chapter. Specifically, we estimate the model with the mobility equation discussed in the last section of chapter 5, and specified in equation (5.7). Recall that C_c is compensation in the current job, including backloading, C_n is the current job compensation, excluding backloading, and C_a is compensation in an alternative job. (If the current job does not have a pension, C_c will be equal to C_n.) Equation (5.7) divides the compensation premium between the current and alternative jobs into two parts, $(\ln C_c - \ln C_n)$ and $(\ln C_n - \ln C_a)$, representing pension backloading and the remainder of the compensation difference, respectively, between the current and alternative jobs. The coefficients of these two parts, which are α_1 and α_2, respectively, are permitted to be free. If the specification captures all of the major influences on mobility, one would expect the coefficients on the pension backloading and compensation premium measures to be similar. The model is estimated with data from the Survey of Income and Program Participation (SIPP) and from the Panel Study of Income Dynamics (PSID).[1]

Results Based on SIPP Data

Table 7.1 presents results from estimating the mobility model with the SIPP data. As the estimates in the columns for the mobility equation indicate, when the parameters for backloading and for the compensation premium are allowed to be free, they are estimated to be fairly close in value. Comparing the log-likelihood values between the constrained version of the model as reported in chapter 6 and the unconstrained version of the model, the hypothesis of equality of these two coefficients is not rejected at any reasonable level of significance.

Table 7.1 Estimates of the Model with Mobility Determined by Separate Measures of Pension Backloading and the Compensation Premium Based on 1984-85 Data from the SIPP

Model component	Mobility equation		Compensation in 1984 job		Compensation in alternative job	
	Marginal effect	(t statistic)	Estimate	(t statistic)	Estimate	(t statistic)
Constant			1.430	(14.79)	0.955	(1.43)
Backloading (α_1)	-0.354	(1.68)	a		a	
Compensation premium (α_2)	-0.304	(2.48)	a		a	
Pension coverage	a		0.342	(17.77)	0.143	(0.81)
Manufacturing	0.005	(0.20)	0.029	(1.45)	-0.007	(0.09)
White collar	0.009	(0.52)	0.073	(2.41)	-0.002	(0.01)
Management/professional	0.008	(0.46)	0.232	(10.25)	0.150	(1.48)
Union status	0.012	(0.71)	0.117	(4.78)	0.023	(0.21)
Firm size > 100	0.012	(0.68)	0.058	(3.04)	-0.036	(0.40)
Years of experience	-0.002	(0.67)	0.000[b]	(0.17)	0.002	(0.23)
Years until retirement	-0.001	(0.40)	-0.003	(1.38)	0.009	(0.98)
Age	0.002	(0.82)	a		a	
Education	-0.002	(0.48)	0.058	(16.65)	0.067	(4.15)
Race (Black)	0.066	(0.67)	-0.189	(4.86)	-0.552	(1.85)
Married	0.009	(0.61)	a		a	
Children under 18	0.009	(0.76)	a		a	

	Eq. 1	Eq. 2	Eq. 3
Home ownership	-0.032 (1.81)		
SMSA	-0.027 (1.02)	0.061[a] (3.41)	0.179[a] (2.41)
Standard deviation of error terms	1.000 --	0.426 (92.35)	0.480 (8.14)
Correlation matrix of error terms	1.000 --	0.734 (2.32) 1.000 --	0.406 (1.06) 0.364 (4.56) 1.000 --
Log-likelihood		-2,304.45	
Number of observations		2,545	

NOTE: Numbers in parentheses are absolute values of asymptotic *t* statistics. See text for descriptions of the dependent variables. The job characteristics in the alternative job equation refer to the characteristics in the initial job, not to the characteristics of the alternative job.
a. Variable is omitted from this equation.
b. Coefficient is less than 0.0005 in absolute value.

This means that, when estimating the model with SIPP data, once a proper measure of the compensation premium is included in the mobility equation, there is no evidence that pension backloading has any greater impact per dollar on mobility than does any other component of the premium.

Comparing the other coefficients in the mobility equation and in the compensation equations to those found in table 6.1, there are no important differences for the constrained version of the model. Notably, the estimate of the compensation differences between pension and nonpension jobs is similar whether or not the compensation differential for work on the current and next best job is decomposed into a measure of backloading and a residual.

Results Based on PSID Data

Table 7.2 presents the analogous results to table 7.1 using data from the 1984-89 PSID. In the mobility equation in table 7.2, the coefficient on the measure of pension backloading(−6.518) is almost one hundred times the size of the coefficient on the remainder of the compensation premium for the pension-covered job (−0.066). The specification is clearly not adequate for fully explaining mobility in the PSID data. These findings are in sharp contrast to the results obtained with the SIPP data.[2]

There are some obvious differences between the PSID and SIPP samples that might account for these variations in findings. One straightforward approach to determining the reason for these differences is to reestimate the PSID results using a one- or two-year mobility period, covering 1984 to 1985 or 1986. We tried to fit the model to this shorter period using the PSID. Such an estimate would reveal any difference in behavior between the earlier and later period or any differences in the pension-mobility relationship between shorter and longer periods. During longer time spans, observed mobility is more often associated with repeated job changes, thereby affecting the observed mobility relationship. However, the estimates for the shorter period would not converge. A probable cause of the problem is that

135

Table 7.2 Estimates of the Model with Mobility Determined by Separate Measures of Pension Backloading and the Compensation Premium, Based on 1984-1989 Data from the PSID

Model component	Mobility equation		Compensation in 1984 job		Compensation in alternative job	
	Marginal effect	(t stat)	Estimate	(t stat)	Estimate	(t stat)
Constant			2.150	(61.75)	2.191	(12.46)
Backloading (α_1)	-6.518	(5.76)	a		a	
Compensation premium (α_2)	-0.066	(0.21)	a		a	
Pension coverage	a		0.237	(6.69)	0.027	(0.21)
Manufacturing	-0.007	(0.10)	0.062	(1.67)	0.215	(1.68)
White collar	0.079	(0.70)	0.060	(0.89)	0.189	(0.60)
Management/professional	0.015	(0.20)	0.235	(5.16)	0.245	(1.32)
Union status	-0.095	(0.66)	0.189	(3.66)	-0.125	(0.75)
Years of experience	-0.005	(0.43)	-0.003	(0.96)	-0.007	(0.66)
Age	0.020	(1.49)	a		a	
Education	0.011	(0.52)	0.070	(8.02)	0.122	(3.50)
Race (Black)	-0.086	(0.70)	-0.266	(3.48)	-0.305	(0.69)
Married	0.002	(0.02)	a		a	
Children under 18	0.014	(0.17)	a		a	
Spouse employment	-0.041	(0.66)	a		a	
Home ownership	-0.211	(2.93)	a		a	

Table 7.2 (continued)

Model component	Mobility equation		Compensation in 1984 job		Compensation in alternative job	
	Marginal effect	(*t* stat)	Estimate	(*t* stat)	Estimate	(*t* stat)
SMSA	0.044	(0.77)	0.090	(2.66)	0.080	(0.61)
Standard deviation of error terms		--	0.334	(32.39)	0.502	(14.43)
Correlation matrix of error terms	1.000	--	0.084	(0.30)	0.094	(0.21)
			1.000	--	0.359	(4.19)
					1.000	--
Log-likelihood			-500.60			
Number of observations			474			

NOTES: Numbers in parentheses are absolute values of asymptotic *t* statistics. See text for descriptions of the dependent variables. The job characteristics in the alternative job equation refer to the characteristics in the initial job, not to the characteristics of the alternative job.
a. Variable is omitted from this equation.

with the fewer observations in the PSID, there is not enough mobility in the data over the shorter period.

Violation of the constraint that coefficients α_1 and α_2 should be close in value may also suggest the existence of some omitted factor in the analysis that is correlated with the measure of pension backloading. The work by Allen, Clark, and McDermed suggests that the omitted factor is not unmeasured worker preference for pension-covered jobs. An obvious question is why the effects of an omitted factor should be evident in the PSID data but not in the SIPP data.

Whatever the reason for the difference in the estimated values of α_1 and α_2 in the PSID sample, it means that the story is not finished. The constraint that a marginal dollar of compensation, regardless of its source, should have the same effect on mobility of the compensation difference is based on strong *a priori* reasoning. Moreover, if the requirement were violated, one would expect the source of the inequality to be liquidity constraints and risk differentials. Both of these factors should cause the effect of a dollar of pension backloading to be weaker than the effect of a marginal dollar of compensation from another source. The data strongly suggest that it is not pension backloading *per se* that holds the individual on the job and accounts for lower turnover on pension-covered jobs. One cannot rule out the possibility that there may be some other factor related to the implicit contract that is correlated with the measure of pension backloading; however, as we have seen, such an omission is not strongly influential in shaping the results from the SIPP data.

NOTES

1. To estimate this model with data from the Survey of Consumer Finances (SCF), it would be necessary to divide equation (5.2) into two parts: one for the backloading and one for the rest of the compensation differential. Both equations would have to be substituted into equation (5.4) to yield an equation analogous to (5.6), and this specification would require two good instruments in order to estimate it. Given that the maximization of the likelihood for the version of the model estimated in chapter 6 occurred along a constraint, it is doubtful that there is sufficient information to allow a satisfactory estimation of the version of the model in which backloading and compensation differential appear as separate arguments.

2. The finding that the pension capital loss variable has a substantially larger coefficient than does a measure of compensation is consistent with results based on the PSID in Allen, Clark, and McDermed (1993), discussed in chapter 3.

Appendix to Chapter 7: PSID Results with Quits Only as the Dependent Variable and with Separate Measures of the Backloading and Compensation Premiums

Appendix Table 7.1 PSID Results of Model with Separate Backloading and Compensation Premium Variables Using Quits as the Dependent Variable

Model component	Mobility equation		Compensation in 1984 job		Compensation in alternative job	
	Marginal effect	(t stat)	Estimate	(t stat)	Estimate	(t stat)
Constant			2.15	(61.21)	2.176	(19.02)
Backloading (α_1)	-6.423	(6.29)	a		a	
Compensation premium (α_2)	0.100	(0.31)	a		a	
Pension coverage	a		0.237	(6.68)	0.018	(0.15)
Manufacturing	-0.065	(0.82)	0.062	(1.67)	0.222	(1.80)
White collar	-0.069	(0.52)	0.060	(0.89)	0.209	(0.62)
Management/professional	0.061	(0.81)	0.235	(5.12)	0.246	(1.32)
Union status	-0.246	(1.57)	0.190	(3.75)	-0.111	(0.67)
Years of experience	-0.004	(0.28)	-0.003	(0.99)	-0.007	(0.66)
Age	0.012	(0.88)	a		a	
Education	0.026	(1.23)	0.070	(7.97)	0.120	(3.63)
Race (Black)	-0.339	(1.67)	-0.266	(3.62)	-0.317	(0.67)
Married	0.069	(0.55)	a		a	
Children under 18	0.018	(0.22)	a		a	
Home ownership	-0.207	(2.62)	a		a	
Spouse employment	0.019	(0.29)	a		a	

139

SMSA	0.028	(0.48)	0.090	(2.65)	0.079	(0.61)
Standard deviation of error term			0.334	(32.85)	0.501	(14.34)
Correlation matrix of error terms	1.000	--	-0.023	(0.07)	0.150	(0.61)
			1.000	--	0.358	(4.53)
					1.000	--
Log-likelihood			-408.16			
Number of observations			474			

NOTES: Numbers in parentheses are absolute values of asymptotic t statistics. See text for descriptions of the dependent variables. The job characteristics in the alternative job equation refer to the characteristics of the initial job, not to the characteristics of the alternative job.
a. Variable is omitted from this equation.

8
Pension Policies and Their Effects

Overview

Backloaded pensions have recently come under scrutiny as possible targets for legislation. A major goal of such reform would be to alter the distribution of payments and incentives in favor of groups of workers who have been shortchanged by backloaded pensions. These include workers whose jobs are terminated through no fault of their own, such as those laid off from pension-covered jobs; women who may leave a pensioned job for family considerations; and possibly individuals who are unable to continue working for health reasons. Another goal of proposed legislation is to insure retirement income for these groups. If workers with typical defined benefit pensions switched jobs midway through their careers, they will have less income during retirement because of the backloading in the first pension. The policy concern is that this reduced income will result in a substantial cut in the standard of living and may even make it more likely that individuals will need public assistance. A third goal is to make it easier for workers to move from declining fields toward more promising growth areas. By providing incentives for workers to stay with their current firms, backloaded pensions can place burdens both on waning industries, which are forced to offer additional incentives to induce workers to leave, and on growing industries, which may have to raise their wages to attract the people they need.

Several policies have been contemplated or enacted to increase the portability of pensions by reducing backloading.[1] For example, the Tax Reform Act of 1986 specifies that, with the exception of multiemployer plans, the period of time for cliff vesting can be no longer than 5 years, as opposed to the previous 10-year maximum. However, since that did not address other pension provisions that cause backloading, the act by itself did not increase portability considerably, except for workers who were hired in their late forties and fifties. Even after 10 years, the value of the pension is only a small fraction of its eventual value for most workers.

To illustrate, recall the figures in table 2.1, which pertain to a worker who is hired at age 25 and retires at age 62. By reducing the vesting period from 10 to 5 years, a 30-year-old worker with 5 years of tenure, who previously would not have been eligible for a pension at all, now qualifies. However, that pension has less than 3 percent of its eventual value, and the present value of the pension is equal to only a couple of weeks' wages. Reducing the vesting period for young workers decreases the size of the backloading to some degree, but a substantial amount of backloading remains. For workers hired closer to retirement, however, the reduction in the vesting period is more important, since there is much less time before the workers begin to collect the pension.

Another policy to enhance the pension values of early leavers is to require that pension benefits be paid on the basis of the projected wage at normal retirement rather than the actual wage at the time of separation. This potential reform has been analyzed by the Congressional Budget Office (1987, pp. 116-17), but as of yet it has not been enacted into law. It would prevent erosion in the value of the calculated benefit that occurs due to inflation between the time workers leave the firm and the time they actually begin to collect the pension.

This policy would also make the vesting period more important. Consider again the worker illustrated in table 2.1. If the required period for vesting is 10 years, then a 30-year-old worker with 5 years of tenure would not have any pension regardless of whether the pension values were calculated based on projected wages or actual wages. With a 5-year vesting period, however, the worker would be eligible for a pension equal to 14 percent (5/37) of its final value if projected wages are used in the calculation, versus 3 percent if actual wages are used.[2] This suggests that the vesting period is a more important issue if pensions are awarded based on projected wages rather than on actual wages.

Still another policy to reduce backloading would be to shift pensions toward defined contribution plans. To some degree, this has already been accomplished, although not intentionally. In 1979, legislation was passed that introduced 401(k) plans, and clarification of their tax status in the early 1980s made these plans very attractive. As a result, the late 1980s and 1990s witnessed an explosive growth of 401(k) plans. Many were added as secondary plans, but a substantial number were introduced as primary plans. It is possible that future legislation will force employers to offer 401(k) or similar plans to their employees. A modest proposal would compel employers who currently provide pensions to at least offer 401(k) plans as supplementary plans if they do not already do so and would force those who do not provide pensions to offer 401(k) plans. A more substantial proposal would require employers who currently offer defined benefit pensions to offer 401(k)-type plans as an alternative. This last proposal would be attractive to new employees. However, it would not be attractive to employees enrolled in defined benefit plans for a period of time, since the previous years of service in the defined benefit plan would still be subject to backloading.

There are a number of possible effects of policies to increase pension portability. The conventional wisdom asserts that backloaded pensions reduce the likelihood that the worker will leave the firm to take another job. It is plausible that firms might want to use backloading in order to save on hiring costs or to recover the costs of training a new employee. Eliminating the incentives provided by a backloaded pension makes it more likely that the worker will leave the firm and that the firm will lose its investment in training and will then have to incur hiring costs to replace the worker. However, it has been the main thrust of this book that this effect is minor. The incentives provided by backloaded pensions are simply not large enough to hold a worker in the face of an alternative job offer, even if that offer involves only a modest wage increase. The correlation between backloaded pensions and low rates of mobility reported in previous studies does not reflect a causal relationship but occurs because of the failure to control for the fact that the job alternatives of workers with pensions are less attractive, relative to their current positions, than the alternatives for workers who do not have pensions.

Another possible effect is on productivity. Some authors have claimed that backloaded pensions are an integral part of a compensation scheme designed to enhance work incentives and increase productivity. The reasoning is that, if workers are caught "shirking," they may be subject to dismissal, which would, in turn, deny them the opportunity to realize the large increases in pension value in the years just before retirement. Evidence on the relationship between deferred compensation and productivity is weak, primarily because productivity is so much harder to measure than mobility. However, our research does suggest that if backloaded pensions reduce shirking and increase productivity, the effect is likely to be rather small as compared to the effects of the other elements of the compensation premium. That is, workers are probably reluctant to engage in activities that may result in dismissal primarily because they could not find another job that pays comparable wages, and only secondarily because they will lose the opportunity to realize large increases in their pension values in the future.

Both with respect to mobility and to shirking, the incentives provided by backloaded pensions are much larger to workers who are within 5 or 10 years of retirement than to their younger co-workers. Our analysis has dealt primarily with workers in their thirties and forties, who have a number of years before retirement. For someone who is only a couple of years away from retirement, increases in pension value represent a much larger percentage of compensation than is the case for younger workers. Thus, although backloaded pensions may not be important determinants of mobility and productivity for workers in general, they may well be a significant factor for older workers.

Funding levels of the plans may also be affected. If a plan is funded on the basis of the benefits for which the company is currently liable, a firm will have to contribute only a relatively small amount towards the pension until the worker nears retirement. If legislation were to require plans to pay benefits on the basis of projected salary, the firm would have to contribute considerably more to cover its commitment. However, the Employment Retirement Income Security Act of 1974 (ERISA) has already encouraged firms to fund pensions on the basis of projected salary, not current salary. Thus, a move toward basing pension calculations on projected salary should not have a large effect, since most firms already fund plans in this way.

A final effect of a move away from backloaded plans is on the distribution of pension payments. In fact, since the effects on mobility, productivity, and funding are likely to be weak, it is likely that this is the most important consequence of such a policy. The most obvious result of a shift from backloaded plans would be to enhance the pensions of workers who change jobs before retirement, particularly workers who hold pensioned jobs early in their careers and then move. However, some amount of caution is needed in analyzing a policy encouraging pension portability, since such a policy may have side effects on groups other than the target population.

The next two sections of this chapter consider the impacts of various approaches to make pensions more portable. A model of the firm and its pension plan is used to simulate the effects of pension policies. Different policies determine the level of pension contributions and, ultimately, the wage of various groups in the firm, even those groups not intentionally affected by the policy. The analysis will focus on redistributive effects, particularly how these policies are likely to influence the wages and pensions of those not targeted as well as those in the targeted group.   In general, we will not be concerned with determining whether government intervention is justified.

A Model of Pension Benefits and Funding

A mechanical approach to the analysis of pension policies would assume that legislation meant to induce certain changes in plan provisions is simply translated into comparable revisions in pensions.[3] This is not likely to be the case. Policies designed to increase pension portability are likely to cause changes in labor costs. Whether or not firms pay a wage premium, that is, whether or not workers are receiving compensation on pension-covered jobs that exceeds their opportunity wage, as long as the amount of compensation is determinate, increases in pension costs will induce adjustments in the remainder of the compensation package. Such adjustments will redistribute pensions and wages among workers who are leaving the firm or retiring at different ages.

In this section we develop a model that is useful for analyzing the first-round responses of firms to changes in pension policies. The model is then used to explore the effects of the various types of legislation that have been or might be adopted to modify the degree of pension backloading in defined benefit plans.

Overall worker productivity is constrained to match overall worker compensation within each period in this model. The firm is also expected to contribute to the pension fund an amount that covers the increase in pension liability, calculated on a projected salary basis.

Management knows that some workers will leave the firm before retirement and that some will stay but does not know which workers are in each group. To allocate the pension contributions among employees, the firm subtracts the same proportion of salary from each worker and pays each person a wage equal to the value of that person's output less the pension contribution. This means that the firm does not necessarily pay each worker an amount equal to the value of that worker's output over the course of his or her employment. Workers who leave the firm early will have more taken out as pension contributions than they ultimately receive as pension benefits, with the reverse being true for workers who stay until retirement. For the workers as a whole, however, the firm does adjust wages to reflect pension contributions, so that total compensation for the group is equal to its output.

In this environment, changes in pension policy that increase the value of some workers' pensions will require the firm to raise the overall contribution rate to the pension fund. With unchanged output, the higher pension contribution will tend to depress somewhat the overall level of wages at the firm. The lower wages will affect other workers as well as those who are receiving the increased pension values. For example, a policy that raises the value of pensions for early leavers may well have the side effect of reducing wages (and hence compensation) for some who stay until they are eligible to retire.

The model we use in this section shows the first-order effects of the policy changes. By first-order effects, we mean the impacts on pension values and wages, not on hiring, retirement patterns, or productivity. Although these first-order results should indicate the major effects on pension values, additional, smaller changes may occur as firms and workers adjust their hiring and retirement behavior in response to the new environment.

In the model, the firm maintains a steady-state labor force. Each year, it hires the same number of 25-year-old workers, half of whom will leave at age 30 and half at the firm's retirement age of 62. The pension plan is characterized by a simple, final-average-salary defined benefit formula. Benefits are 1 percent of the average of the final salary times years of credited service. Although this generosity coefficient is somewhat low in comparison with reported data, the pension benefit formula does not include a social security offset that would otherwise reduce the value of the pension. For an employee who joins the firm at age 25, retires at age 62, and dies at age 80 (the presumed age of death of all workers in the model), a generosity coefficient of 1 percent leads to a pension with a present value at the time of hire that is a little over 10 percent of the present value of the wage stream. In comparison with available data (Gustman and Steinmeier 1989), the 10 percent ratio is slightly low but not unreasonable.

The plan is funded so as to cover its liabilities on a projected liability basis. For those currently employed, the projected liability is calculated as a prorated share of the present value of the pension that would be paid if half of the workers remained with the firm until retirement and the other half left after five years. That is, management is assumed to know the distribution of separation ages but not necessarily which workers will leave early and which workers will stay until retirement. The prorated share is the ratio of the present value of the wage paid to date divided by the present value of the wage to be paid over the full term of attachment.

To finance the pension plan, the firm first must calculate the amount of contributions needed each year to maintain the level of funding just described. The firm then compares the level of contributions to the total value of the output of its labor force in a given year and calculates a contribution rate as a percentage of that value. This contribution rate is applied uniformly to all workers who are employed at the firm that year, and each worker is paid a wage that is equal to the difference between the value of his or her output and the amount of the pension contribution. The calculations allow for the feedback effect of wages on the amount of the pension liability, so that, in fact, the contribution rate and wages are determined simultaneously.

This type of financing is consistent with available evidence regarding the relationship between wages and increments in pension values. Certainly, for an individual worker, compensation does not appear to match productivity on a year-by-year basis. We have seen that pension accrual profiles are characterized by sharp spikes at the time that benefits become vested, and that there are even sharper spikes when the worker satisfies the eligibility requirements for early or normal retirement benefits. At these times, there does not appear to be an offsetting depression in wages. In conjunction with fairly smooth presumed growth in productivity, the relatively even growth of wages, despite the jumps and dips in the accrual pattern of pensions, suggests that if workers pay for pensions in the form of reduced wages, the path of these payments is also comparatively smooth over time.

One final premise has been noted but warrants some further discussion. The assumption that the productivity of workers is fixed, particularly with respect to changes in the rules governing pensions, runs counter to many of the explanations as to why pensions have the specific defined benefit form observed for most plans. These explanations usually involve the effect of the plans on overall productivity. However, at this time there is no consensus as to whether pensions affect productivity and, if so, by how much, and almost all of the current hypotheses are not fully consistent with the empirical evidence. (See Gustman and Steinmeier 1989b; Gustman and Mitchell 1992; Gustman, Mitchell, and Steinmeier 1994.)[4] In the absence of agreement on this issue, the following analysis ignores any effect of changes in pension rules on productivity. For similar reasons, the analysis only addresses the change in the pension contribution rates necessary to keep the plans funded, rather than other revisions in pension plans by firms in response to policy changes.

Effects of Potential Pension Policies on the Distribution of Compensation

Using the model just outlined, this section presents the results of simulations evaluating policies designed to increase pension portability. The firm is assumed to have been hiring the same number of workers for a long enough time to have achieved an equilibrium, and the pension is also assumed to have been in existence sufficiently long for its financing per worker to be in equilibrium. For these simulations, productivity in the base year is assumed to be $20,000 per worker, growing at the rate of 6 percent per year (in nominal terms). This projection of wage growth is consistent with rates used by the Congressional Budget Office (CBO) for the late 1980s (1987, p. 154) and with postwar experience. The interest rate used in these calculations is 6 percent, which is about 1 percentage point lower than the estimate used by the CBO.

Effect of Earlier Vesting

One approach to improving the situation of early leavers is to require earlier vesting. The first two columns of data in table 8.1 show the situation with 10-year cliff vesting. In order to finance the pensions of the half of the individuals who stay until retirement, the firm must make contributions equal to approximately 9.5 percent of payroll. For both the short-tenure workers and the long-tenure workers, these pension contributions (line 2 of the table) are subtracted from productivity to yield wages. The workers who stay until retirement get pensions whose present value is 10.8 percent of the present value of their wages. The remaining 1.3 percent is financed by the workers who leave at age 30, who make pension contributions but receive nothing in return.

The vesting period is shortened to five years in the middle two columns. With this change, all of the workers are now eligible for pensions. Instead of not receiving a pension at all, the short-tenure workers now receive a pension with a present value that amounts to 1.7 percent of their wages. This is much lower than the percentage received by workers who stay until retirement because the final (nominal) wage is used in the pension formula. Note that because the short-tenure workers now receive some pension benefits, the contribution rate to the pension plan has risen from 9.5 percent to 9.7 percent of payroll. This increase is borne mostly by the workers who stay until retirement, causing both their wages and pensions to decline. Because the pensions of the short-tenure workers are so small, however, the compensation reduction of the long-tenure workers is minor, amounting to only 0.2 percent of their lifetime compensation.

Effect of Using Projected Wages in the Pension Formula

Even if one's benefits are fully vested, pension benefits received by early leavers are worth proportionately less than the benefits of those who stay to retirement. A mechanical reason for this result is that benefits for early leavers are calculated using the wage at separation rather than the wage that would be received had the worker stayed until normal retirement (Bulow 1982). Requiring that an employer use the wage projected to the normal retirement age would eliminate the loss due to using the current nominal wage in computing benefits for terminated,

Table 8.1 Policies to Assist Early Leavers

Benefit factors	10-year vesting using actual wage at separation		5-year vesting using actual wage at separation		5-year vesting using projected wage at retirement	
	Leave at 30	Retire at 62	Leave at 30	Retire at 62	Leave at 30	Retire at 62
Productivity	$100,000	$740,000	$100,000	$740,000	$100,000	$740,000
- Pension contribution	8,708	64,439	8,874	65,669	9,770	72,296
= Wages	91,292	675,561	91,126	674,331	90,230	667,704
+ Pension benefits	0	73,147	1,529	73,014	9,770	72,296
= Total compensation	91,212	748,708	92,655	747,345	100,000	740,000
Pension/wage ratio	0	0.108	0.017	0.108	0.108	0.108
Compensation/productivity ratio	0.913	1.012	0.927	1.010	1.000	1.000

NOTE: All dollar amounts are the present values of the corresponding streams, discounted back to the base year.

vested employees under a defined benefit plan. The last two columns of table 8.1 show the result of such a policy. When there is full vesting and the projected wage at normal retirement instead of the current wage is used in calculating benefits for early leavers, the pension value for the short-tenure workers rises to $9,770. This is the amount that results when there is no pension backloading. Backloading is inherent in using the nominal wage at the time of separation to calculate pension benefits; this practice reduces the present value of the pension for early leavers by about 84 percent as compared to a nonbackloaded pension (comparing $1,529 to $9,770).

In this case, the pension contribution has gone up to about 10.8 percent. The higher pension contribution affects everyone, but whereas the short-tenure workers recoup the increased pension contributions (and more) with enhanced pension benefits, the long-tenure workers incur drops in both wages and pensions. As compared with the middle columns of table 8.1, wages for long-tenure workers are lower by over $6,600, and the pension is lower by over $700. The net effect of using projected wages in the benefit formula is to redistribute over $7,300 from each long-tenure worker to each short-tenure worker. More precisely, the high-tenure workers lose the $7,300 subsidy that had been given to them by the practice of using backloaded pensions. This $7,300 transfer represents over 7 percent of the total compensation of the low-tenure workers but only about 1 percent of the total compensation of the high-tenure workers.

Effect of Changing to Defined Contribution Pensions

If the firm had a defined contribution plan with a contribution rate of 10.8 percent, the figures in equilibrium would look exactly like the figures in the last two columns of table 8.1. The long-tenure workers would not be as well off as with backloaded pensions, but they would still be paid an amount equal to their value of their output. If a firm with a defined benefit pension offers workers the opportunity to convert to a defined contribution pension, it is fairly clear that workers who are anticipating a short stay at the firm will be ahead by making the change. For longer-term workers, however, the conclusion will depend to some extent upon the specifics of the offer. If the wages to be used in the defined benefit calculation were the unadjusted nominal wages at the time of conversion, long-tenure workers would incur the equivalent of a pension capital loss if they converted and would have strong incentives to remain with the defined benefit plan. If the wages to be used were wages at retirement, the decision of the long-tenure workers would depend upon the level of the pension contribution of the defined contribution plan relative to the generosity of the defined benefit formula. Another determinant would be the degree to which the individual values the defined benefit pension's annuity aspect, which is likely to be absent from a defined contribution plan.

Other Considerations

The analyses reported in this chapter pertain to stylized pension plans. We have tried to select plan parameters that, on the basis of our previous research, are representative. Nevertheless, the examples are much simpler than most of the plans encountered in our empirical work. Moreover, the effects of these various policies will depend on the actual employment mix within the firm, whether employment is growing or shrinking, and expected patterns of turnover.

There are features of pension plans, in addition to vesting requirements and the choice of wage used in the formula, that affect pension portability. Eligibility requirements for normal retirement based on years of service and actuarial bonuses for early retirement raise the penalty on early leavers. Such provisions increase the value of the pensions of other groups and hence the contribution rates of all. Also, there are many idiosyncratic features of pensions affecting incentives for mobility. Frequently, a single plan uses different formulas in calculating benefits for terminated vested workers, early retirees, and normal retirees. Indeed, the choice of formula used for calculating normal retirement benefits may vary with the years of service accumulated by the worker. Using the projected wage in the pension formula would not eliminate these influences on portability, and any effort to make pensions fully portable would have to take these plan features into account.

In sum, the recent easing of vesting requirements will not provide much additional protection to early leavers. Eliminating the backloading of pensions will have a greater effect. Furthermore, neither policy is likely to have much of an impact on the incentives for turnover for workers in the first decades of attachment to the firm.

Caveats for Pension Policy Analysis

If we had found that pension backloading provided strong disincentives to mobility, especially at young ages, it would suggest that backloading of defined benefit pensions meets one of the necessary conditions for a firm to have adopted pensions as a device for regulating mobility, presumably to increase productivity and/or reduce labor costs. Also, if we had found that defined benefit pensions were important in determining the incentives for turnover, and the extent of turnover, we would add one more building block to our understanding of the factors underlying the reasons for pension plans and for their specific characteristics. It could then be asserted with some confidence that the features of the pension, such as backloading, play an important role in determining a number of outcomes of interest.

Our findings suggest, however, that backloaded pension plans have a smaller effect on the incentives relevant to mobility decisions than the literature has implied. Our research also suggests that the relationship of the cost of mobility to observed mobility behavior is weaker than that indicated by the conventional literature. A further conclusion is that pensions are not likely to be a major tool for influencing mobility, and thus it is unlikely that mobility considerations are an important motivation for the adoption of defined benefit plans by firms.

None of this means that pension characteristics are unimportant to pension recipients who experience turnover from their jobs at different ages. In addition, a fundamental concern of policy makers is the distribution of retirement incomes, which is affected by the turnover experience of covered workers. What our findings do suggest is that an analysis of the relationship of pension plan provisions to pension incomes may safely disregard the impact of pension changes on mobility. More broadly speaking, our analysis suggests that policy makers may be less concerned with the effects of pension regulation on mobility and productivity than they might otherwise be.

Of course, pension legislation has had a number of goals in addition to the ones cited above. One objective is to recognize and protect a form of the pension contract under the law so as to increase the likelihood that a worker who is promised a benefit will receive it, as well as to raise the fraction of the promised pension that is paid when the full commitment is not delivered. Another, more recent, goal is to encourage those who wish to work beyond the plan's normal retirement age, so as to mitigate the funding crises in social security and medicare. There also is a desire to secure comparable treatment for low-wage workers employed by firms offering generous pensions to their high-wage workers. Another major aim is to extend pension coverage as widely as possible. Finally, Congress has been giving more weight to controlling the revenue loss resulting from the favorable tax treatment of pensions.[5]

These goals may produce initiatives that will reinforce policies to limit backloading or work counter to such policies. For instance, workers who want to stay beyond the normal retirement age are hurt by rules that mandate projected wages in pension formulas, but they may be helped by policies that require the crediting of age and years of service or the actuarial adjustment of benefits for employees who continue working. When the compensation budget is constrained, efforts to help certain classes of workers may have negative impacts on other classes of workers. Those individuals who are adversely affected are often the target of additional policies designed to improve their status or the incentives they face. Consequently, different policies may have conflicting effects, and compatibility among goals becomes an issue.

NOTES

1. A survey of major policies to increase portability that were considered in the past is presented in Turner (1993, chapter 9).

2. With projected wages, the only difference between the pension value at age 30 and its final value occurs because different tenure lengths are used in the formula. The 14 percent figures comes from dividing the 5 years of tenure at age 30 by 37 years of tenure at age 62. The 3 percent figure comes from column 6 of table 2.1.

3. A number of exercises along these lines performed by Hay/Huggins are described in chapter 9 of Turner (1993).

4. Explanations for defined benefit pensions typically focus either on the advantages of benefit backloading for the design of efficient compensation schemes or on the importance of the retirement incentives that these plans create, thereby increasing firm profitability. In the former group,

one explanation is that the backloading of defined benefit plans discourages shirking by workers and thereby increases productivity. However, given the accrual patterns of pension plans, the potential pension loss from separation is greatest in the middle years of tenure at the firm. As we discussed in chapter 3, it is unclear why incentives against shirking need to be so much stronger in the middle years than in the early or later years. Another explanation proposed by Oi (1983), that pensions help to screen out early quitters and hence to reduce hiring and training costs, faces similar objections. Again, if the goal is to recover training costs incurred early in the employment relationship, it is unclear why the firms should make the cost of leaving less in the early years than in the middle years. Further doubts about shirking and training cost explanations for pensions come from evidence that indicates a poor understanding of plan incentives, not only by the workers (Gustman and Steinmeier 1989a; Mitchell 1988), but by their employers (Kotlikoff and Wise 1987b). Firms that use pensions to create incentives against mobility and shirking have good reason to insure that these incentives are well understood.

The other category of explanations for pensions influencing productivity focuses on retirement incentives. In a model discussed by Parsons (1983), older workers are characterized by a much wider dispersion of productivity than are younger workers. Either because the firms cannot distinguish well which older workers are productive and which are not, or because firms are unable to act on this knowledge, they find it more efficient not to employ workers past a certain age. In this explanation, pensions provide workers with the incentives to retire at the appropriate age, thereby increasing overall productivity. The major drawback of this rationale is its failure to account for the large number of plans in which eligibility for retirement depends partly, if not entirely, on years of service. For example, there are plans that permit retirement with full benefits after 30 years of service, regardless of age. If the goal of pensions is to induce retirement at an appropriate age, then it would seem that eligibility for retirement should be based on age, not on years of service.

5. For a useful discussion of pension policies and their origins, see CBO (1987, appendix A).

9
Conclusions

It is a widely accepted view that pensions reduce labor mobility. Observing that mobility is lower on pension covered jobs and that defined benefit pension plans backload benefits, many students of the pension-mobility relationship have concluded that it is the disincentive created by backloading that decreases mobility. Others have reached this conclusion on the basis of more careful empirical analysis, as indicated in our survey of the literature.

In the preceding chapters, we have examined the basis for this view. Our research provides evidence that is strongly inconsistent with the thesis that lower mobility on pension-covered jobs is due to backloading of defined benefit plans.

A direct examination of defined benefit pension formulas indicates that backloading accounts for only a small portion of the value of the future pension. We have shown that, on average, a worker in his thirties or forties requires a raise of only a few percentage points to overcome the loss from pension backloading. While pension backloading may amount to half a year's earnings in a sample of prime-aged male workers, those in the sample have a remaining worklife of decades, so that even a modest wage increase will generate earnings that can overcome the one-time loss from leaving a job with a backloaded pension.

An analysis of worker mobility in three separate data sets also raises questions about the idea that backloading accounts for lower mobility from pension-covered jobs. In particular, reduced form multivariate mobility equations indicate that the reduction in mobility from pension-covered jobs is the same whether the worker is covered by a defined benefit plan, which is backloaded, or by a defined contribution plan, which is not.

If pension backloading does not explain the lower mobility from pension-covered jobs, then what is causing the reduced mobility in these cases? Much of the analysis in this book has focused on the hypothesis that pension-covered jobs offer higher wages than do non-pensioned jobs and that this is done for unobserved reasons, including the payment of efficiency wages or rents. Thus, the compensation premium received by workers on jobs that offer pensions accounts for the associated lower mobility.

This explanation has been supported in analyses using data from three surveys: the Survey of Consumer Finances (SCF), the Survey of Income and Program Participation (SIPP), and the Panel Study on Income Dynamics (PSID). The descriptive information from these surveys suggests that higher wages are paid on pension-covered jobs than on other jobs. The value of the pension widens the compensation difference. The descriptive data also indicate that wage losses are greater for movers from pension-covered jobs; these losses are augmented because the new jobs frequently do not offer pensions.

Estimates of a model in which the three outcomes (mobility, compensation on the current job, and compensation on the next best job) are jointly determined support the idea that it is the higher compensation on pension-covered jobs that accounts for lower mobility from those jobs. The analysis suggests that because the value of backloading is just a small fraction of the compensation differential for those who hold pension-covered jobs, backloading plays only a very slight role in explaining the mobility differences between those with and without pensions. For pension-covered workers, most of the difference in mobility is associated with the higher compensation on their current as opposed to next best job.

To test the idea that pension backloading and compensation differentials between the current and next best job fully account for the mobility differences between workers with and without pensions, a model was specified in which mobility was a function of separate coefficients for pension backloading and the compensation premium. We then tested the constraint that a dollar's worth of pension backloading has the same effect on turnover as a dollar's difference in compensation from other sources. In one data set, the SIPP, coefficients measuring the effect of backloading and of other compensation differences were found to be approximately equal, with no significant differences. This test suggests that there is no important omitted factor in the model. However, in a second data set, the PSID, the estimated coefficients were significantly different, with a much higher coefficient for a variable measuring backloading, suggesting that there may be a factor not captured in the estimated models. Although the results from these tests are mixed, the small size of the pension incentives compared to the other elements of compensation leads us to favor the SIPP results.

In the end, we have very strong evidence that lower mobility on pension-covered jobs is not a result of the backloading of defined benefit pension plans. Much of the available evidence also points to the conclusion that turnover is lower from pension-covered jobs because they offer incumbents higher compensation than is available in alternative employment. There also is some suggestion that an unmeasured factor associated with employment on jobs offering backloaded pensions may account for part of the reduction in turnover observed for pension-covered workers, although it is unclear why the effect of the unobservable element is much stronger in the PSID than in the SIPP data. It will be the task of future researchers to determine exactly how much there is to that story.

References

Abraham, Katherine and Henry S. Farber. 1985. "Length of Service and Promotions in Union and Nonunion Work Groups," *Industrial and Labor Relations Review* 38 (3): 408-420.

_____. 1987. "Job Duration, Seniority and Earnings," *American Economic Review* 77(3): 278-297.

Akerlof, George A., and Lawrence F. Katz. 1989. "Workers' Trust Funds and the Logic Of Wage Profiles," *Quarterly Journal of Economics* 114: 525-536.

Allen, Steven G., Robert L. Clark, and Ann A. McDermed. 1987. "Pensions and Lifetime Jobs: The New Industrial Feudalism Revisited." Final Draft Report, U.S. Department of Labor.

_____. 1991. "Pensions, Bonding and Lifetime Jobs." National Bureau of Economic Research, Working Paper No. 3688.

_____. 1992. "Post-Retirement Benefit Increases in the 1980's." In *Trends In Pensions* 1992, John Turner and Daniel J. Beller, eds., Washington, DC: Government Printing Office.

_____. 1993. "Pension Bonding and Lifetime Jobs," *Journal of Human Resources* 28 (3): 463-481.

Allen, Steven G., Robert L. Clark, and Daniel Sumner. 1986. "Post Retirement Adjustments of Pensions," *Journal of Human Resources* 21(1): 118-137.

Altonji, Joseph, and Robert Shakotko. 1987. "Do Wages Rise with Job Seniority?" *Review of Economic Studies* 54: 437-459.

Barnow, Burt S. and Ronald G. Ehrenberg. 1979. "The Costs of Defined Benefit Pension Plans and Firm Adjustments," *Quarterly Journal of Economics* 93: 523-540.

Bartel, Ann P., and George J. Borjas. 1977. "Middle-Age Job Mobility: Its Determinants and Consequences." In *Men in Their Preretirement Years*, Seymour Wolfbein, ed. Philadelphia: Temple University.

Becker, Gary S. 1964. *Human Capital.* New York: Columbia University Press.

Beller, Daniel J., and Helen H. Lawrence. 1992. "Trends in Private Pension Coverage." In *Trends In Pensions 1992*, John Turner and Daniel J. Beller, eds., Washington, DC: Government Printing Office.

Ben Porath, Yoram. 1967. "The Production of Human Capital and the Life Cycle of Earnings," *Journal of Political Economy* 75: 352-365.

Berndt, Ernst, Brownyn Hall, Robert Hall, and Jerry Hausman. 1974. "Estimation and Inference in Nonlinear Structural Models," *Annals of Economic and Social Measurement* 3: 653-665.

162

Board of Governors of The Federal Reserve System. Surveys of Consumer Finances. 1983 and 1989.

Brown, Charles C. 1980. "Equalizing Differences in the Labor Market," *Quarterly Journal of Economics* 94(1): 113-134.

Brown, Charles, and James Medoff. 1989. "The Employer Size Wage Effect," *Journal of Political Economy* 97: 1027-1059.

Bulow, Jeremy I. 1981. "Early Retirement Pension Benefits." National Bureau of Economic Research, Working Paper No. 654.

———. 1982. "What Are Corporate Pension Liabilities?" *Quarterly Journal of Economics* 97(3): 435-452.

Cain, Glen. 1976. "The Challenge of Segmented Labor Market Theories to Orthodox Theory: A Survey," *Journal of Economic Literature* 14(4): 1215-1257.

Clark, Robert L. and Ann A. McDermed. 1990. *The Choice of Pension Plans in a Changing Regulatory Environment*. Washington, DC: American Enterprise Institute.

Congressional Budget Office. 1987. *Tax Policy For Pensions And Retirement Savings*. Washington, DC: Government Printing Office.

Dickens, William T. and Lawrence F. Katz. 1987. "Inter-Industry Wage Differences and Industry Characteristics." In *Unemployment and the Structure of Labor Markets,* Kevin Lang and Jonathan Leonard, eds. London: Basil Blackwell.

Dorsey, Stuart. 1987. "The Economic Functions of Private Pensions: An Empirical Analysis," *Journal of Labor Economics* 5 (part 2): S171-89.

Dorsey, Stuart, Christopher Cornwell, and David Macpherson. 1994. "Pensions, Training and Productivity." Paper presented at a research conference, Miami University.

Economic Report of The President. Various dates.

Even, William E., and David A. Macpherson. 1992. "Pensions, Labor Turnover and Employer Size." Unpublished paper, Oxford, Ohio, May.

Farber, Henry S. 1993. "The Incidence and Costs of Job Loss: 1982-1991." *Brookings Papers on Economic Activity: Microeconomics.*

Gibbons, Robert, and Lawrence F. Katz. 1989. "Does Unmeasured Ability Explain Inter-Industry Wage Differentials?" National Bureau of Economic Research, Working Paper No. 3182.

———. 1991. "Layoffs and Lemons," *Journal of Labor Economics* 9(4): 351-380.

Gordon, Roger H., and Alan S. Blinder. 1980. "Market Wages, Reservation Wages and Retirement," *Journal of Public Economics* 14: 277-308.

Gustman, Alan L., Olivia S. Mitchell. 1992. "Pensions and Labor Market Activity: Behavior and Data Requirements." In *Pensions and the Economy,*

Zvi Bodie and Alicia Munnell, eds. Philadelphia: Pension Research Council, University of Pennsylvania Press.

Gustman, Alan L., Olivia S. Mitchell, and Thomas L. Steinmeier. 1993. "Retirement Research Using the Health and Retirement Survey." National Bureau of Economic Research, Working Paper No. 4813.

_____ . 1994. "The Role of Pensions in the Labor Market." *Industrial and Labor Relations Review* 47 (3): 417-438.

Gustman, Alan L., and Thomas L. Steinmeier. 1987. "Pensions, Efficiency Wages and Job Mobility." National Bureau of Economic Research, Working Paper No. 2426.

_____ . 1989a. "An Analysis of Pension Benefit Formulas, Pension Wealth and Incentives from Pensions." *Research in Labor Economics* 10: 33-106.

_____ . 1989b. "Evaluating Pension Policies in a Model with Endogenous Contributions." National Bureau of Economic Research, Working Paper No. 3085.

_____ . 1990. "Pension Portability and Labor Mobility." Report to the U.S. Department of Labor.

_____ . 1991. "The Effects of Pensions and Retirement Policies on Retirement in Higher Education," *The American Economic Review: Papers and Proceedings* 81(2): 111-115.

_____ . 1992a. "The Stampede towards Defined Contribution Pension Plans: Fact or Fiction?" *Industrial Relations* 31(2): 361-369.

_____ . 1992b. "Pension Incentives, Mandatory Retirement and Retirement Behavior in Higher Education," *Economics of Education Review* 11(3): 195-204.

_____ . 1993a. "Cost of Living Adjustments in Pensions." In *As the Workforce Ages: Costs, Benefits And Policy Challenges,* Olivia S. Mitchell, ed. Ithaca: Cornell University Press.

_____ . 1993b. "Pension Portability And Labor Mobility: Evidence from the Survey of Income and Program Participation," *Journal of Public Economics* 50: 299-323.

Hay/Huggins Company, Inc. 1988. *Pension Plan Cost Study.* Washington DC, Pension Benefit Guaranty Corporation.

Hutchens, Robert. 1986. "Delayed Payment Contracts and a Firm's Propensity to Hire Older Workers," *Journal of Labor Economics* 4: 439-457.

Ippolito, Richard A. 1986. *Pensions, Economics and Public Policy.* Pension Research Council. Homewood, IL: Dow Jones-Irwin.

_____ . 1987. "Why Federal Workers Don't Quit," *Journal of Human Resources* 22(2): 281-293.

_____ . 1993. "Selecting and Retaining High Quality Workers: A Theory of 401k Pensions." Unpublished paper, April.

_____ . Forthcoming a. "Toward Explaining the Growth of Defined Contribution Pension Plans," *Industrial Relations.*

_____ . Forthcoming b. "Pensions and Indenture Premia," *Journal of Human
Resources.*

Jovanovic, Boyan. 1979a. "Job Matching and the Theory of Turnover," *Journal of Political Economy* 87: 972-990.

_____ . 1979b. "Firm-Specific Capital and Turnover," *Journal of Political
Economy* 87: 1246-1260.

Katz, Lawrence F. 1988. "Some Recent Developments in Labor Economics
and their Implications for Macroeconomics," *Journal of Money, Credit and
Banking* 20 (3) part 2: 507-522.

Katz, Lawrence F., and Lawrence H.Summers. 1989. "Industry Rents: Evidence and Implications," *Brookings Papers on Economic Activity: Microeconomics.*

Kotlikoff, Laurence J., and David A. Wise. 1985. "Labor Compensation and
the Structure of Private Pension Plans: Evidence for Contractual vs. Spot
Labor Markets." In *Pensions, Labor, and Individual Choice,* David A. Wise,
ed. Chicago: The University of Chicago Press.

_____ . 1987a. "The Incentive Effects of Private Pension Plans," In *Issues in
Pension Economics,* Zvi Bodie, John B. Shoven, and David A. Wise eds.
Chicago: University of Chicago Press.

_____ . 1987b. "Employee Retirement and a Firm's Pension Plan." National
Bureau of Economic Research, Working Paper No. 2323.

Krueger, Alan B., and Lawrence Summers. 1987. "Reflections on the Inter-
Industry Wage Structure." In *Unemployment and the Structure of Labor
Markets,* Kevin Lang and Jonathan Leonard, eds. London: Basil Blackwell,
1987.

_____ . 1988. "Efficiency Wages and the Interindustry Wage Structure,"
Econometrica 56(2): 259-293.

Kruse, Douglas L. Forthcoming. "Pension Substitution in the 1980's: Why the
Shift Toward Defined Contribution Pension Plans?" *Industrial Relations.*

_____ . 1993. *Profit Sharing: Does It Make a Difference?* Kalamazoo, MI:
W.E. Upjohn Institute.

Lazear, Edward P. 1979. "Why is There Mandatory Retirement?" *Journal of
Political Economy* 87(6):1261-1284.

_____ . 1983. "Pensions as Severance Pay." In *Financial Aspects of the
United States Pension System,* Zvi Bodie and John B. Shoven, ed. Chicago:
University of Chicago Press.

Lazear, Edward P., and Robert L. Moore. 1988. "Pensions and Mobility." In
Pensions in the U.S. Economy, Zvi Bodie, John Shoven, and David Wise,
eds. Chicago: University of Chicago Press.

Light, Audrey. 1994. "Transitions from School to Work: A Survey of Research Using the National Longitudinal Surveys." U.S. Department of Labor, Bureau of Labor Statistics.

McCormick, Barry, and Gordon Hughes. 1984. "The Influence of Pensions on Job Mobility," *Journal of Public Economics* 23: 183-206.

Mincer, Jacob B. 1974. *Schooling, Experience and Earnings.* New York: Columbia University Press.

Mitchell, Olivia S. 1982. "Fringe Benefits and Labor Mobility." *Journal of Human Resources* 17(2): 286-298.

_____ . 1983. "Fringe Benefits and the Cost of Changing Jobs," *Industrial and Labor Relations Review* 37: 70-78.

_____ . 1988. "Worker Knowledge of Pension Provisions," *Journal of Labor Economics* 6(1): 28-39.

Montgomery, Edward, Katherine Shaw and Mary Ellen Benedict. 1992. "Pensions and Wages: an Hedonic Price Theory Approach," *International Economic Review* 33(1): 111-128.

Oi, Walter. 1983. "The Durability of Worker-Firm Attachments." Mimeograph. University of Rochester.

Parsons, Donald. 1983. "The Industrial Demand for Older Workers". Mimeograph. The Ohio State University.

Petersen, Mitchell A. 1992. "Pension Reversions and Worker Stockholder Wealth," *Quarterly Journal of Economics* 107(3): 1033-1056.

President's Commission on Pension Policy. 1981. *Coming of Age: Toward a National Retirement Income Policy.* Washington, DC: Government Printing Office.

Ross, A. 1958. "Do We Have a New Industrial Feudalism?" *American Economic Review* 48(5): 918-922.

Salop, Joanne, and Steven Salop. 1976. "Self Selection and Turnover in the Labor Market," *Quarterly Journal of Economics* 90: 619-627.

Schiller, Bradley, and Randall D. Weiss. 1979. "The Impact of Private Pensions on Firm Attachment," *Review of Economics and Statistics*: 369-380.

Segal, Martin. 1986. "Post-Institutionalism in Labor Economics: The Forties and Fifties Revisited," *Industrial and Labor Relations Review* 39(3): 388-403.

Slichter, Sumner. 1950. "Notes on the Structure of Wages," *Review of Economics and Statistics* 32: 80-91.

Stock, James H., and David A. Wise. 1990. "Pensions, the Option Value of Work, and Retirement," *Econometrica* 58(5): 1151-1180.

Topel, Robert. 1986. "Job Mobility, Search and Earnings Growth: A Reinterpretation of Human Capital Earnings Functions," *Research in Labor Economics* 8: 199-223.

_____ . 1990. "Specific Capital, Mobility, and Wages: Wages Rise with Job Seniority." National Bureau of Economic Research, Working Paper No. 3294.

Turner, John A. 1993. *Pension Policy for a Mobile Labor Force*. Kalamazoo, MI: W.E. Upjohn Institute.

U.S. Department of Labor, Bureau of Labor Statistics. National Longitudinal Surveys of Labor Market Experience. Center for Human Resource Research, The Ohio State University. Various dates.

U.S. Government Printing Office. The Board of Trustees, Federal Old-Age and Survivors Insurance and Disability Insurance Trust Fund. Annual Report, various years.

U.S. Department of Commerce, Bureau of the Census. Survey of Income and Program Participation. Various dates.

U.S. Department of Labor, Bureau of Labor Statistics. 1964. "Labor Mobility And Private Pension Plans." Bulletin No. 1407.

U.S. Department of Labor, Bureau of Labor Statistics. 1992. "How Workers Get Their Training: A 1991 Update." Bulletin No. 2407.

INDEX

About the Institute

The W.E. Upjohn Institute for Employment Research is a nonprofit research organization devoted to finding and promoting solutions to employment-related problems at the national, state, and local level. It is an activity of the W.E. Upjohn Unemployment Trustee Corporation, which was established in 1932 to administer a fund set aside by the late Dr. W.E. Upjohn, founder of The Upjohn Company, to seek ways to counteract the loss of employment income during economic downturns.

The Institute is funded largely by income from the W.E. Upjohn Unemployment Trust, supplemented by outside grants, contracts, and sales of publications. Activities of the Institute are comprised of the following elements: (1) a research program conducted by a resident staff of professional social scientists; (2) a competitive grant program, which expands and complements the internal research program by providing financial support to researchers outside the Institute; (3) a publications program, which provides the major vehicle for the dissemination of research by staff and grantees, as well as other selected work in the field; and (4) an Employment Management Services division, which manages most of the publicly funded employment and training programs in the local area.

The broad objectives of the Institute's research, grant, and publication programs are to: (1) promote scholarship and experimentation on issues of public and private employment and unemployment policy; and (2) make knowledge and scholarship relevant and useful to policymakers in their pursuit of solutions to employment and unemployment problems.

Current areas of concentration for these programs include: causes, consequences, and measures to alleviate unemployment; social insurance and income maintenance programs; compensation; workforce quality; work arrangements; family labor issues; labor-management relations; and regional economic development and local labor markets.